MVVM in Delphi

Architecting and Building
Model View ViewModel
Applications

John Kouraklis

Apress®

MVVM in Delphi: Architecting and Building Model View ViewModel Applications

John Kouraklis
London, United Kingdom

ISBN-13 (pbk): 978-1-4842-2213-3   ISBN-13 (electronic): 978-1-4842-2214-0
DOI 10.1007/978-1-4842-2214-0

Library of Congress Control Number: 2016956108

Managing Director: Welmoed Spahr
Lead Editor: Steve Anglin
Technical Reviewer: Nick Hodges
Editorial Board: Steve Anglin, Pramila Balan, Louise Corrigan, Jonathan Gennick,
     Robert Hutchinson, Celestin Suresh John, Michelle Lowman, James Markham,
     Susan McDermott, Matthew Moodie, Jeffrey Pepper, Douglas Pundick, Ben Renow-Clarke,
     Gwenan Spearing
Coordinating Editor: Mark Powers
Copy Editor: Kezia Endsley
Compositor: SPi Global
Indexer: SPi Global
Artist: SPi Global

Distributed to the book trade worldwide by Springer Science+Business Media New York, 233 Spring Street, 6th Floor, New York, NY 10013. Phone 1-800-SPRINGER, fax (201) 348-4505, e-mail orders-ny@springer-sbm.com, or visit www.springeronline.com. Apress Media, LLC is a California LLC and the sole member (owner) is Springer Science + Business Media Finance Inc (SSBM Finance Inc). SSBM Finance Inc is a **Delaware** corporation.

For information on translations, please e-mail rights@apress.com, or visit www.apress.com.

Apress and friends of ED books may be purchased in bulk for academic, corporate, or promotional use. eBook versions and licenses are also available for most titles. For more information, reference our Special Bulk Sales–eBook Licensing web page at www.apress.com/bulk-sales.

Any source code or other supplementary materials referenced by the author in this text are available to readers at www.apress.com/9781484222133. For detailed information about how to locate your book's source code, go to www.apress.com/source-code/. Readers can also access source code at SpringerLink in the Supplementary Material section for each chapter.

Printed on acid-free paper

To my parents, who demonstrated breadth of mind and a sense of vision when they bought me my first computer in times when computers were in their infancy in my country and they were considered a "bad influence" on kids by many.

Contents at a Glance

About the Author xi

About the Technical Reviewer xiii

Introduction xv

■Chapter 1: MVVM as Design Pattern 1

■Chapter 2: Setting Up the POSApp 13

■Chapter 3: MVVM as Design Philosophy 43

■Chapter 4: Two-Way Communication 59

■Chapter 5: Converting the InvoiceForm 79

■Chapter 6: User Interaction 105

■Chapter 7: Input Validation 125

Index 143

Contents

About the Author xi

About the Technical Reviewer xiii

Introduction xv

▉Chapter 1: MVVM as Design Pattern 1

Three-Tier Application Architecture 2

Model-View-Controller (MVC) 3

Model-View-Presenter (MVP) 6

Model-View-ViewModel (MVVM) 7

Summary 11

References 11

▉Chapter 2: Setting Up the POSApp 13

POSApp Forms 14

Mixing Business and Presentation 22

Declaration of Classes 22

The Database Unit 23

Total Sales 26

The Main Form 28

The Sales Invoice Form 29

    Retrieving Data 32

    Updating the Form 35

Summary 42

References 42

Chapter 3: MVVM as Design Philosophy 43

The View of the MainScreen 43

The Model of the MainScreen 45

The ViewModel of the MainScreen 48

Creating the Classes 51

How the Code Works 52

Creating the ViewModel and the Model Outside the Main Form 53

Notes About the Code 55

How We Converted MainScreen 57

Summary 58

Chapter 4: Two-Way Communication 59

The Provider-Subscriber (ProSu) Framework 60

Two-Way Communication (Revisited) 65

Making the Code More Efficient 71

Summary 77

References 77

Chapter 5: Converting the InvoiceForm 79

The View of the InvoiceForm 79

The Model of the InvoiceForm 82

The ViewModel of the InvoiceForm 85

Retrieving the Labels from the ViewModel 87

Setting Up the Invoice Form 90

Disabling and Hiding Elements 98

Getting the Customer and Items Lists 101

Summary 103

■Chapter 6: User Interaction 105

Selecting a Customer 105

Adding an Item to the Invoice 112

The Model 112

The ViewModel 115

The View 119

Summary 124

■Chapter 7: Input Validation 125

Checking Inputs 125

Bits and Pieces 130

Deleting an Item from the Invoice 130

Applying Discounts to the Invoices 132

Printing the Invoice and Closing the Form 137

Summary 142

Index 143

About the Author

John Kouraklis started exploring computers when he was 16. He started developing IN Delphi, as a hobby, initially, and then as a professional activity. He developed a wide range of applications, from financial software to reverse engineering tools and, more recently, discovered the fascinating world of cross-platform development.

About the Technical Reviewer

Nick Hodges is a Senior Software Engineer at Gateway Ticketing Systems, a firm that provides ticketing and access control systems to the largest amusement parks, zoos, and museums around the world.

Nick is a software developer at heart. He's been a Pascal/Delphi developer for over 20 years and still thinks that Delphi is the best development tool out there. He loves to read programming books, attend conferences, and watch cool videos about new programming techniques. He generally tries to be an industry thought leader.

Introduction

The wide use of portable devices (tablets, smart phones, and smart watches) and the connectability between them gave rise to a whole new challenge to software development. Cross-platform programming, or the production of applications that target more than one platform, is getting momentum as the new wave of software development. Under these circumstances, professionals must preserve resources (time, skills, infrastructure, human capital, and knowledge) and maximize output while developing for multiple target platforms. Companies and professionals have responded to this development by offering new tools that facilitate the development of cross-platform applications.

Delphi FireMonkey framework is such a tool. It allows the development of cross-platform applications using Delphi; an incarnation of Object Pascal and one of the strongest and well developed programming languages available to developers. However, having a tool is not enough to produce efficient cross-platform applications. Although it makes programming easier and perhaps makes developing user interfaces on different devices trivial, it does not answer the question about how we can design our software in such way that cross-platform operations—such as moving across platforms, switching data providers, and injecting new platform-dependent implementations of algorithms—can be done with maximum flexibility and quality and minimum expense to programming effort and time.

These thoughts give strong support to programming patterns and, in particular, to design patterns, which is the overall concept of this book. Design patterns take us one step before designing the front-end GUI; they open the angle and perspective from which we see our applications and force us to think in a modular way.

The ModelView-View-Model (MVVM) design pattern is characterized by its flexibility and adaptability to different situations under diverse conditions. This book attempts to open the field of MVVM to Delphi developers. It saves deep theoretical discussions and conceptual analysis for other types of publications and focuses on the practicalities of implementing a Delphi framework according to the guidelines of MVVM. At the same time, the book develops a methodology about how to convert an application that doesn't follow a design pattern to one that complies to the MVVM paradigm.

As always, in the field of software development, there are hardly universal solutions applicable to every situation; there are rather efficient solutions for specific problems. The code in this book and the suggestions offered serve as a foundation to help you make your own choices about the version and implementation of MVVM that suits your needs, your company's requirements and policies, and the specifications of the applications you are developing. For sure, there are areas where you can apply more sophistication and abstraction to the design and others that simpler approaches exist.

Who This Book Is For

The book focuses on the busy Delphi developer with good knowledge of Object Pascal. Although the code has been developed using Delphi, it doesn't rely on specific features that cannot be found in other versions of Object Pascal (including standard forms and visual elements). Therefore, the value that can be gained expands the Delphi domain and falls into the broader area of Object Pascal.

After reading this book you will be able to:

- Identify the different aspects of the Model-ModelView-View (MVVM) design pattern.

- Design applications based on the MVVM approach.

- Implement the different elements of the framework in Delphi in ways that suit your application needs.

- Undertake the task of converting existing applications to meet the MVVM design.

The Development Environment

The code in this book was developed using the following environment:

- Embarcadero Delphi 10 Seattle Architect

- Microsoft Windows 7 Professional

- FireMonkey framework

I use the Architect edition of Delphi, but this is not a requirement. You can use whichever version of Delphi you have access to. I use FireMonkey but, again, everything we discuss in this book is applicable to VCL as well. If the VCL approach is different, I flag this in the code. As mentioned, the code in this book uses pure Object Pascal which, in turn, means you can use different versions of development environments like Lazarus and the like. Lastly, if linking to the graphical interface (forms and views) is not your concern or priority, you can develop a console application using the ViewModel and Model classes as they are presented in this book, without any modifications. That is the first hint to the simplicity and power of the MVVM pattern.

The Book's Structure

This book has seven chapters. While you are going through the chapters, you will be exploring different aspects of MVVM and your knowledge will gradually build to cover common situations found in rich content applications.

Chapter 1: MVVM as Design Pattern

This chapter builds on your understanding of the MVVM framework. It briefly visits different presentation patterns in a historical manner with the sole purpose of showing how the approach to presentation patterns shifted toward MVVM.

Chapter 2: Setting Up the POSApp

In this chapter, we create POSApp. This is a simple application that resembles more sophisticated invoicing systems. We will build the application in such way that it doesn't respect any design patterns. In the following chapters, we rely on POSApp to demonstrate the implementation of the MVVM pattern.

Chapter 3: MVVM as Design Philosophy

In this chapter, we start exploring the MVVM pattern by first looking at a way to organize the different aspects of POSApp as they are understood by MVVM. This is the first time where we see the flexibility, clean separation of the different parts, and loose communication. We also see how communication is achieved between the different parts of the MVVM design.

Chapter 4: Two-Way Communication

This chapter expands on the previous chapter and implements a way to accomplish bidirectional communication between the MVVM components without jeopardizing the principals of loose connections. At the end of this chapter, we formalize the methodology to convert non-MVVM application to follow the paradigm.

Chapter 5: Converting the Invoice Form

Chapter 5 continues with the development of the most complex form of the POSApp. In this chapter, we apply the methodology we developed in Chapter 4. This chapter offers a systematic way to approach legacy (or monolithic) applications when you want to convert them to modern patterns.

Chapter 6: User Interaction

The content of this chapter deals with how we can manage user interactions (mouse clicks, popup menus, and so on) with respect to the MVVM and generate responsive actions.

Chapter 7: Input Validation

The last chapter of the book deals with how to use the MVVM framework to check on inputs by the user, as in the case of an edit field. We will also complete the conversion of POSApp by developing some secondary actions such as a close and cancel button.

Code Files

This book comes with Delphi code files. You can download the code from the publisher's web site at this address: http://www.apress.com/9781484222133. For convenience, I include Table 1, which lists the project names per chapter and a short description.

Table 1. *Project Names Per Chapter as Found in the Book's Code Files*

Chapter	Project Name	Notes
2	POSApp	
3	POSAppMVVM	The viewmodel and the model are created inside the main form
	POSAppMVVMMainForm	The viewmodel and the model are created outside the main form
4	POSAppMVVMMainFormTest	Test application for the ProSu framework
	POSAppMVVMMainFormInterfaces	POSApp uses interfaces as it appears in the chapter
	POSAppMVVMMainFormFullInterfaces	POSApp is fully converted to use interfaces
5	View.InvoiceForm.fmx View.InvoiceForm.pas	Empty invoice form
	POSAppMVVMStart	Implements the invoice form with dummy variables
	POSAppMVVMInvoiceForm	Implements all the changes in Chapter 5
6	POSAppMVVMUserInteraction	Implements user interaction
7	POSAppMVVMFinal	Final version of POSApp (converted to MVVM)

CHAPTER 1

■ ■ ■

MVVM as Design Pattern

Presentation patterns are already an old story. Although it is difficult to identify who introduced them, it looks like the seminal programming language SmallTalk dating back to the 1970s is responsible for making one of the first presentation patterns popular; the Model-View-Controller (MVC) design (Kay, 1993; Timms, 2014).

Krasner and Pope (1988) offered a formalized description of the MVC pattern and they basically influenced a generation of programmers who appreciated the merits of keeping apart what appears in the frond-end of an application and what is happening behind the scenes. As the authors state,

> *"Isolating functional units from each other as much as possible makes it easier for the application designer to understand and modify each particular unit"*

—Krasner and Pope (1988)

There are three take-aways from the above statement, first, the separation in the design; then this separation needs be as strong as possible giving independent units and, lastly, the reason for the proposed separation. The developers are able to see clearly what each unit is doing and to alter their behavior.

Keeping functions apart creates an environment where changes to different parts of an application can be performed in a controlled manner, with bugs being spotted and fixed more easily. At the same time, it forces a specific mindset where developers think of applications in a modular way. Put simply, this means that software is developed in units and parts that are linked together with very strict but simple rules to the level of abstraction. This concept is usually described with the term *separation of concern* (SoC) and it is one of the most important concepts in modern software development and presentation patterns.

Electronic supplementary material The online version of this chapter (doi:10.1007/978-1-4842-2214-0_1) contains supplementary material, which is available to authorized users.

© John Kouraklis 2016
J. Kouraklis, *MVVM in Delphi*, DOI 10.1007/978-1-4842-2214-0_1

■ **Note**   A *concern* in computer science is a group of activities and data that represent different but related functionalities in a piece of software. A *separation of concerns* (SoC) is a school of thought in which the code is split into several distinct concerns, with minimal overlapping (coupling). If you are not familiar with SoC or you need to refresh your knowledge, visit these general resources (Wikipedia, n.d.; Greer, 2008.) and check this video for a presentation about how SoC fits in object oriented programming and service oriented architectures Lilleaas, 2013).

The benefits you get with such loose connections include the ability to better test, move, and share units among different projects with minimal, if not zero, modifications. Reusability becomes the way to preserve resources (development time and effort) and engineer highly maintainable code.

Three-Tier Application Architecture

Although this breakdown of functionality has been introduced in design patterns, such an approach has been widely used in enterprise applications. It has materialized into what is known as a three-tier architecture. According to this approach, there are three tiers (or layers) in applications:

- *Presentation layer*: The user interface (UI) that shows data to the user and represents states or different forms of data

- *Business layer*: This part deals with data validation and business rules and norms

- *Data Access layer*: A mechanism that connects the application to the medium of choice to store data

It is important to realize that these layers are not just tags we put on sections or files in our application in order to group them together. Earlier we identified that the separation in the design serves different functionalities. Those layers are a way to encapsulate the logic that each part performs. Logic is different from data and data itself is different from information. Data in the form of raw elements (e.g., product price, bank account transactions or discount rate) can move across layers and appear in any of them, and each layer can capture data and interpret it in a way that makes sense to each layer. At this stage, data has been transferred to information. For example, if you consider the discount rate a customer is eligible to enjoy and the price of a product, both pulled from a database, you are just dealing with "data". Now, if you want to apply the discount to the price of the product the customer ordered, you contextualize that data and generate information.

Both elements (data and information) may appear in any of the aforementioned layers, depending on layer's functionality (see Figure 1-1). Logic can be seen as the tangible version of information; in this example, the logic would be to multiply the discount rate and the price of the product. Logic can also be seen as the programming code that appears in the layers.

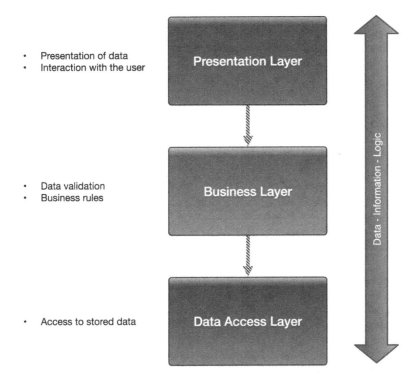

- Presentation of data
- Interaction with the user

Presentation Layer

- Data validation
- Business rules

Business Layer

- Access to stored data

Data Access Layer

Data - Information - Logic

Figure 1-1. *Three-tier application structure*

Presentation patterns form a different constellation of the tasks performed in an application. They tend to identify a clear front-end that is accessed by a user (the View). Then, the patterns define the part of the application that deals with data, the information (to use the previous term) and programming logic. This part is usually called the Model. A question that arises at this stage is how the communication between the View and the Model is achieved. Many approaches have been proposed and today we have a group of solutions that form the MV* family of patterns.

In the next sections, we are going to visit two of the most prominent members: the Model-View-Controller (MVC) and the Model-View-Presenter (MVP). This book doesn't discuss those patterns extensively. Instead, it covers the fundamentals before concentrating our attention on the Model-View-ViewModel (MVVM) pattern.

Model-View-Controller (MVC)

The Model-View-Controller (MVC) pattern includes three parts: the Model, the View, and the Controller. The Model represents the state of the application (not only the state of data) and, obviously, sets up and maintains any communication with databases and other sources of data. The View is pretty straightforward. It defines what the user sees and gets from the application. This may include the user interface and different forms of exported data (CSV or HTML files, for example). The Controller receives events from the view and passes them to the Model. The Model processes the events and the View synchronizes itself with any changes that occur in the Model (see Figure 1-2).

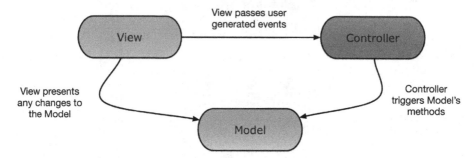

Figure 1-2. *The Model-View-Controller (MVC) pattern*

Figure 1-2 indicates that the controller is aware of the existence of the Model and, in most cases, of the View, as well. The View is aware of the Controller and the Model. The Model works as a detached and separate entity that exhibits the biggest separation of functionality. A typical problem in the implementation of the MV* patterns is the order of creation of the parts and the responsibility for this. In the most common MVC approach, the Controller is responsible for creating the Model and choosing the View.

Thinking in terms of the three-tier architecture, you may notice that the mapping between the MVC components and those in the three-tier design is not straightforward, as there is an overlap of functions and tasks. Figure 1-3 shows how the two patterns are related.

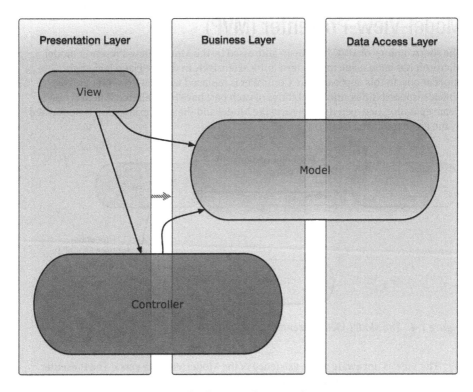

Figure 1-3. *Relationship between the three-tier design and MVC*

MVC is widely used to generate rich user interfaces. It is quite popular on the web and the Android operating system implements this pattern (da Silva, 2014). The introduction of the Model as a component with loose connections to the other components implements a clear separation of concerns. Developers can test the View and the Controller as separate entities.

However, the interaction between the View and the Controller and their link to the Model blur the separation among the View, the state of the application, and the state of the View. For example, if you want to change the color of an edit field because the user entered a wrong value, you need to contact the Controller for the user input, observe the Model for the validation, and implement programming logic in the View in order to change the color of the field based on the outcome of the validation. This "state of the view" spans across the different layers of the pattern and it demonstrates that a good level of coupling still exists. This, in turn, introduces a transferability issue. If you want to replace the current View with an alternative one, you need to develop the Controller again (Vice and Siddique, 2012).

Model-View-Presenter (MVP)

The shortcomings of MVC have been addressed by the Model-View-Presenter model. Microsoft has been using this pattern quite extensively in the WPF and Silverlight applications. In this approach, the Controller is replaced with the Presenter and the duties, responsibilities, and capabilities of each part have been altered. There is now a clear separation between the View and the Model and the synchronization is performed by the Presenter (see Figure 1-4).

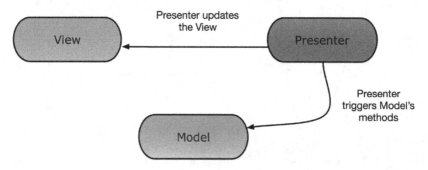

Figure 1-4. *The Model-View-Presenter (MVP) pattern*

The View is not aware of the existence of the Model and vice versa. The Presenter has a pivotal role, as it receives user inputs from the View, handles mapping between the View and the Model, and performs complex business logic (Syromiatnikov, 2014). The Presenter is typically created first. Using the previous example with the color of the edit field, the validation is performed in the Presenter and the View is updated using a number of setter methods. The Presenter is now responsible for providing the correct color to the view.

■ **Note**   The version of MVP pattern presented here indicates there is no communication between the View and the Model. This is commonly referred as *Passive View*. There is an alternative implementation of MVP that allows for communication between the View and the Model, but it has limited scope. This is called *Supervising Controller*. See Martin Fowler's web site for a detailed presentation of the two implementations (Fowler, 2006a; 2006b).

Figure 1-5 shows the three-tier structure for the MVP pattern.

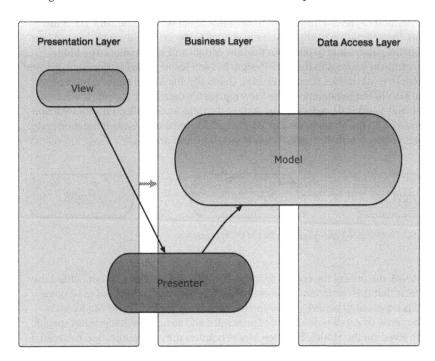

Figure 1-5. *Relationship between the three-tier design and MVP*

This time, the Presenter has moved deeper in the business layer. This is because the Presenter is responsible for much of the validation and it keeps most of the state of the View. The Model is unchanged in this version. The three elements are less interlinked and this link is based on more flexible structures (interfaces). This arrangement offers better testability, as the Model and the View can be replaced by mock units or by different implementations.

Apart from these benefits, developers find that while the user interface becomes more sophisticated, there is the need for more code. More code means more opportunities for bugs and an increase in the effort needed to maintain the code base.

Model-View-ViewModel (MVVM)

MVVM came as an alternative to MVC and MVP patterns. SmallTalk introduced this framework in the 1980s, initially under the name *Application Model* and later using the name *Presentation Model* (Vice and Siddique, 2012). Most of the arguments that support MVVM are based on the the fact that the View and the View's state in the previous approaches (MVC/MVP) are still interlinked to the Model to a degree that individual testing is hard to be achieved. This linkage interferes with the general principle of modular programming.

In the MVVM pattern, the ViewModel replaces the Presenter and the Controller. The responsibilities of the ViewModel and the View are now different.

It is common to present the MVVM pattern in a linear way (Figure 1-6). The reason behind this constellation is to emphasize the change to the tasks that are performed from each part of the pattern and to point out the flow of data and information. The Model remains mainly the same as in the MVP design. It is still responsible for accessing different data sources (e.g., databases, files, or servers). Generally, the Model tends to be very thin in the MVVM implementation. The View represents data in the appropriate format (graphical/non-graphical), reflecting the state of the data, and it collects user interaction and events. As with the Model, Views in MVVM include minimum implementation code, only what is required to make the View work and allow user actions.

Figure 1-6. *The Model-View-ViewModel (MVVM) pattern*

In MVVM, the bulk of the code is found in the ViewModel. The concept behind the ViewModel is that this component represents the way the view is expected to be (view state) and is expected to behave to user interactions (view logic). It is *the Model of the View* in the sense that it describes a set of principles and structures that present specific data as retrieved via the Model. The ViewModel handles the communication between the View and the Model by passing all the necessary data from the View to the Model in a form that the Model can digest. Validation is performed in the ViewModel component.

In this pattern, the components work in sets of two. The View is aware of the ViewModel, updates the ViewModel's properties, and tracks any changes that occur in the latter. The ViewModel is not aware of the existence of the View. This one-way awareness justifies the linear presentation of the pattern in Figure 1-6, which is also found in many books and articles. In a similar way, the model is not aware of the viewmodel (or the view itself) but it is, only, the viewmodel which has access to the model. The ViewModel passes events and data to the Model, as they are pushed by the view in forms that the Model can interpret. The ViewModel tracks any changes created by the Model and, consequently, pushes to the View any necessary signals according to View and the business rules.

In many articles and presentations of the MVVM pattern, authors often attempt to discuss the one-way relationships between the components by implying that the View and the ViewModel are interchangeable or that they perform equivalent actions. For example, Timms (2014) states that "In MVVM, the view believes that the ViewModel is its view".

Let me clarify the meaning of this statement, as it can have a number of design implications if it is misinterpreted. As mentioned, the View is aware of the ViewModel but the ViewModel is not aware of the View. If you follow the above statement, the View sees the ViewModel as the tunnel that visualizes or expresses what is taking place in the View. In addition, it indicates that the View can perform filtering or transformations according to the required View logic. This is not the case with the MVVM pattern, because the ViewModel is responsible for the job "behind the scenes of the view". Moreover, a view can very easily react to, connect to, and visualize several ViewModels, whereas a ViewModel models only one view.

Consider the case of a rowing machine that uses a performance monitor to show various forms of data to the athlete. For the purpose of this example, I used screens from the Concept2 rowing machine (see Figure 1-7).

All Data

Force Curve

Pace Boat/Skier

Figure 1-7. *Different screens of the performance monitor of the Concept2 rowing machine (Courtesy of Concept2, Inc; used with permission)*

As the athlete pulls the handle, force is transmitted to the internal mechanism of the machine. This mechanism has a circular construction that's free to rotate around its perpendicular axis. The rowing machine allows the athlete to rotate the internal circular mechanism according to the force and the pace he or she is exercising to the handle. In addition, the machine has an instrument that receives the heartbeats of the athlete. All these technical parts provide the required elements (the variables) to the machine in order to start making calculations, such as elapsed time, consumed calories, speed, etc.

If we attempt to look at the rowing machine under the MVVM paradigm in an educational approach, what the equipment does is to implement the model of the rowing machine (application), which represents a dynamic state of "raw data". The performance monitor can be considered as a collection of different views of the model. What you need in between is a way to transform data in forms that reveal meaningful information to the athlete. For example, you need to take the rotation speed of the internal mechanism and the elapsed time (as supplied by the model) and translate them to the distance the athletes would cover if they were rowing in a real boat. This transformation of data is the job of the ViewModel in the MVVM domain.

The screen (view) of Concept2 reveals several pieces of information (e.g., elapsed time, strokes per minute, estimated time to cover 500m, distance covered, heartbeats, and projected distance for current speed). Depending on the complexity of the calculations and the connections between them, they can be seen as information provided by different ViewModels. Figure 1-8 shows one possible architecture.

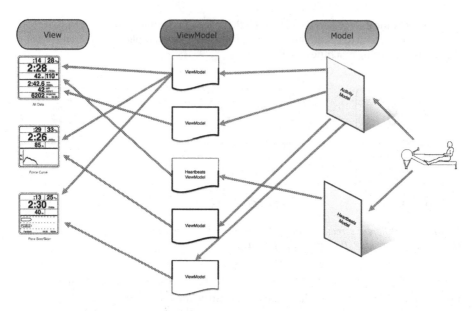

Figure 1-8. *A MVVM approach to the performance computer of Concept2 rowing machine*

In this design, you have two models (one that deals with data for the physical activity and one that captures the heartbeats of the athlete). These models are used by a number of ViewModels that produce different graphical interpretations (view models) of the data. For example, the second screen has a part that shows the elapsed time and the speed and another part that shows the force curve. What the MVVM approach has done is allow you to understand which part of the application does what and to create loose connections between the processing of data and information and the way they are presented to the users. One point worth noting is that the design shown in the figure is not the only one you can implement. This is one of the strengths of the MVVM approach; it allows you to devise ViewModels that fit your Models and Views instead of having to adjust your Views (and perhaps your Model) to the pattern, as is often the case with the other options in the MV* domain.

In terms of the three-tier architecture, now the Model has been pushed deeper to the data layer, as it mostly deals with data (see Figure 1-9). It still covers aspects of the business layer, as many times transformation of data is required at business level. The View resides in the presentation layer like before and the ViewModel is now charged with a wider range of activities and, therefore, occupies both the presentation and the business layers. The presentation side of the figure captures the fact that the ViewModel implements the logic and state of the View and the business layer corresponds to any logic that allows the manipulation of data in ways that serve the View's logic.

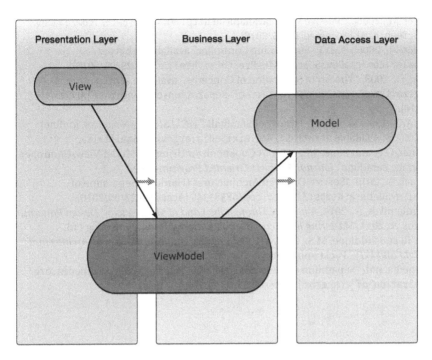

Figure 1-9. *Relationship between the three-tier design and MVVM*

Obviously, this is a generalized description of the relationship between the MVVM parts and the three-tier architecture. Different applications, needs, and requirements and different schools of thought in the MVVM universe may position the Model and the ViewModel closer to the business layer, as the discussion about the alternative designs of the Concept2 case has shown.

Summary

This chapter visited the most common design patterns and attempted to create a link to the three-tier architecture design of enterprise software. One of the key points is that MVVM is very flexible and developers can implement it following more than one designs. This flexibility is one of the strong points of the pattern. What follows is an implementation of such a design. The next chapter develops a sample application and the rest of the book shows you how to apply the MVVM paradigm.

References

da Silva, L.P., 2014. "Model-driven GUI generation and navigation for Android BIS apps." Model-*Driven Engineering and Software Development* (MODELSWARD), 2014 2nd International Conference on IEEE, pp.400–407.

Fowler, M., 2006a. "Passive View," available at http://martinfowler.com/eaaDev/PassiveScreen.html [Accessed 29/05/2016].

Fowler, M., 2006b. "MVP: Supervising Controller," available at http://martinfowler.com/eaaDev/SupervisingPresenter.html [Access 29/05/2016].

Greer, D., 2008. "The Art of Separation of Concerns," available at http://aspiringcraftsman.com/2008/01/03/art-of-separation-of-concerns/ [Accessed 25/05/2016].

Kay, A.C., 1993. "The Early History of Smalltalk," *ACM SIGPLAN Notices*, [online] 28(3), pp.69–95. Available at <https://en.wikipedia.org/wiki/Smalltalk>.

Krasner, G.E. and Pope, S.T., 1988. "A Cookbook for Using the Model-View-Controller User Interface Paradigm". *Journal of Object-Oriented Programming*.

Lilleaas, A., 2013. "Service Oriented Architectures (Hardcore Separation of Concerns)", available at https://vimeo.com/68383348 [Accessed 27/05/2016].

Syromiatnikov, A., 2014. *A Journey Through the Land of Model-View-* Design Patterns*.

Timms, S., 2014. *Mastering JavaScript Design Patterns*. Packt Publishing Ltd.

Vice, R. and Siddique, M.S., 2012. *MVVM Survival Guide for Enterprise Architecture in Silverlight and WPF*. Packt Publishing.

Wikipedia, n.d. "Separation of Concerns", available at https://en.wikipedia.org/wiki/Separation_of_concerns [Accessed 25/05/2016].

CHAPTER 2

■ ■ ■

Setting Up the POSApp

As described in the introduction, in this book we will work on how to convert an application to follow the MVVM pattern. The example application is a POS client for purchasing clothes. The first version will use an approach that mixes the user interface and the model of the application (the business logic). This type of design is referred as *monolithic* and it is pretty much what you have when you deal with so-called *legacy code,* especially if your application was created in the 1980s and 1990s.

■ **Note**   You come across monolithic design in old applications (legacy) but you can also end up with such a structure if you follow tightly the development workflow in Rapid Application Development (RAD) environments, such as the IDE that comes with Delphi. RAD makes very easy to write code for an event generated by a GUI element and access data-aware components (non-GUI elements) in one line. This ease of coding creates a mindset of tight design between the model and the presentation of an application. In turn, this contradicts the philosophy of the presentation patterns. For more details about the pros and cons of RAD environments and the implied methodologies, see Begel (2007) and Gerber (2007).

Let's call this application POSApp. The requirements for POSApp are the following:

- The user can create an invoice for a sale.

- The user can choose customers by name and see their outstanding balances and discount rates (based on predefined rates per customer). There is also a "Retail Customer" for general (anonymous) sales.

- The user can add and remove items in the invoice for each sale and adjust the quantities.

- The user can apply the relevant discount rate.

- The user can see the total amount of sales.

© John Kouraklis 2016
J. Kouraklis, *MVVM in Delphi*, DOI 10.1007/978-1-4842-2214-0_2

POSApp Forms

POSApp has two screens. The main screen (see Figure 2-1) shows the Total Sales and includes a button that allows users to issue an invoice.

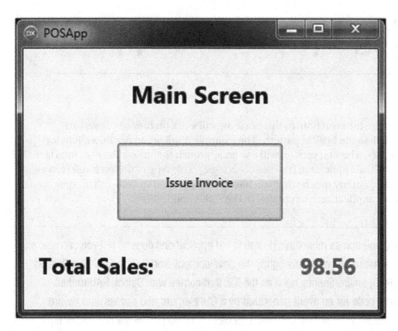

Figure 2-1. *The main screen of the POSApp*

The second screen is more complicated and can be seen in Figure 2-2. It includes a popup menu to allow the users to select a customer. They can then see the outstanding balance of the customer and the discount rate that he or she is entitled to enjoy.

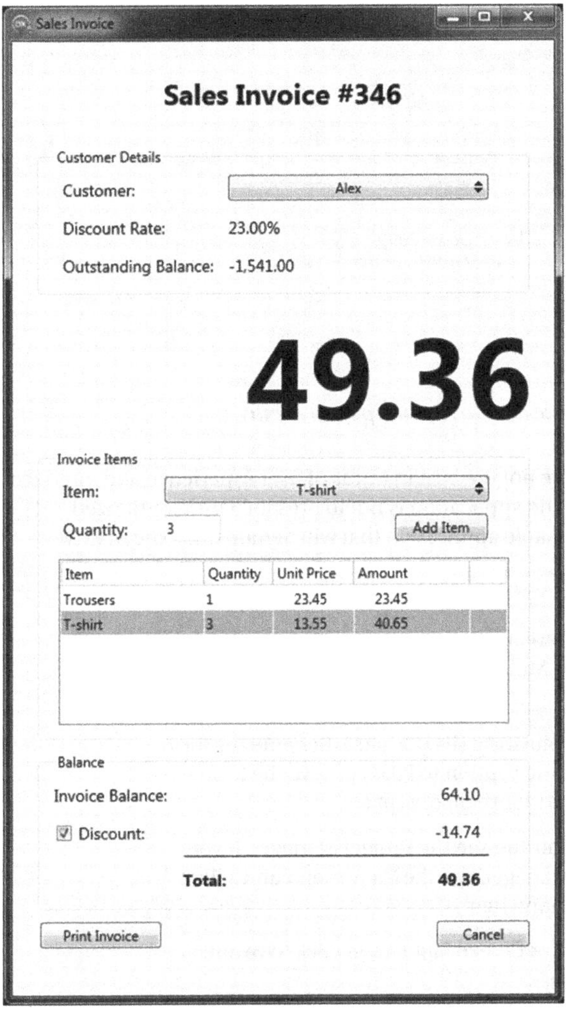

Figure 2-2. *The invoice screen of POSApp*

There is also a region in the form where the user selects the items to sell and sets the quantity. If users want to delete an item from the invoice, a popup is revealed when they right-click on the items list (see Figure 2-3). The current balance is shown; users can print the invoice or cancel it.

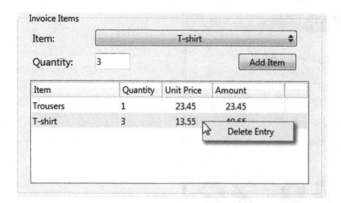

Figure 2-3. *Right-click on an invoice item to reveal a popup menu*

If you think that the screens are not the best in terms of user experience and interface design, you are right. The point of the application is not to present a nice, optimized user interface but to provide a workable application that will demonstrate the MVVM framework.

Let's start building POSApp.

1. Open Delphi IDE and create a new blank multi-device project (choose File ➤ New ➤ Multi-Device Application ➤ Blank Application).

2. Your project has only one form (Unit1.pas). Rename the form MainForm and change the caption to POSApp. Save the form and give it the name MainScreenForm.pas.

3. In the right-side bar, you can see the Project Manager. If you can't see the Project Manager, use the View menu and select the Project Manager menu item.

4. Right-click on the Project1.exe label, then click Save and enter the name POSApp.

5. Right-click on the ProjectGroup1 label in the Project Manager and select Save Project Group. Save the project under the name POSAppProjectGroup. It is very likely that you'll see a different number in the ProjectGroup label. This doesn't affect the code here and you can continue with the next steps.

6. Add three TLabel components and one TButton to the MainForm.

7. Rename the components and edit their properties according to Figure 2-4.

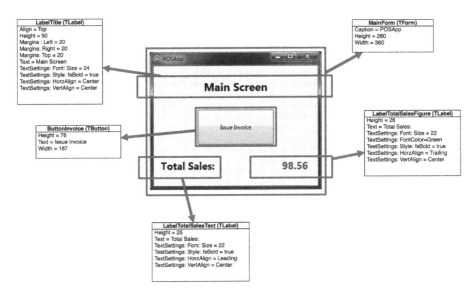

Figure 2-4. Components and their properties of the MainScreenForm

8. Add a second multi-device form to the project. An alternative way to do this instead of the process in Step 1 is to right-click on the POSApp.exe element in the Project Manager (see Figure 2-5) and choose HD Form from the wizard.

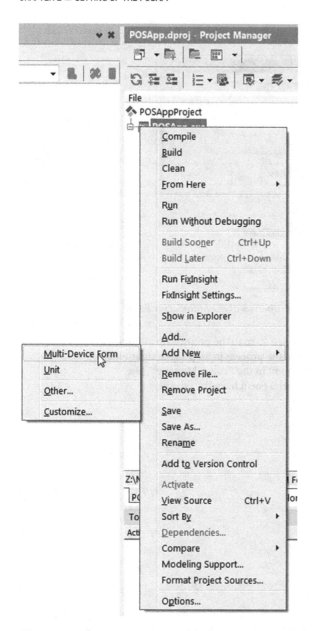

Figure 2-5. *The popup menu to add a form to the project*

9. Name the form SalesInvoiceForm and save it as
   InvoiceForm.pas. Then use Figure 2-6 to add components,
   rename them, and adjust their properties.

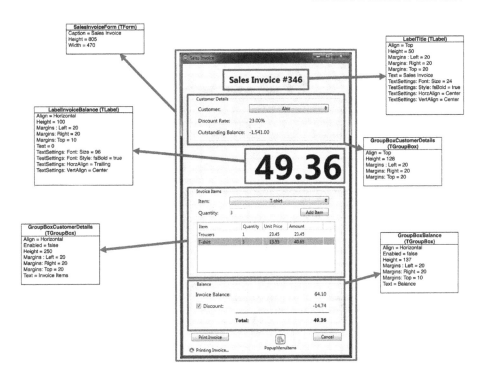

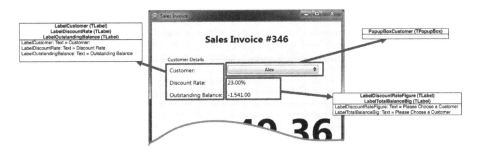

Figure 2-6. *The Components of the InvoiceForm and their properties*

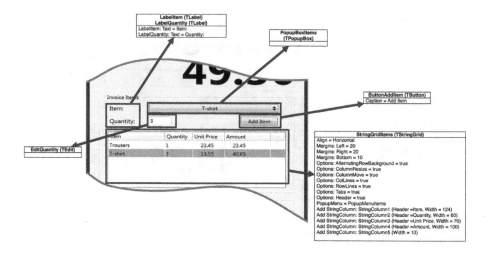

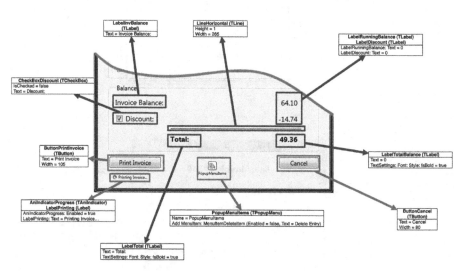

Figure 2-6. (*continued*)

At this stage, we have created the user interface for your application. Use the Project
➤ Options menu option and click Forms. Then, select the InvoiceForm from the left side
list and use the relevant button to transfer it to the list on the right, as shown in Figure 2-7.
This will prevent the application from creating the InvoiceForm automatically. You can also
remove the following code from InvoiceForm.pas. We will create the forms manually.

```
var
    SalesInvoiceForm: TSalesInvoiceForm;
```

Remove this

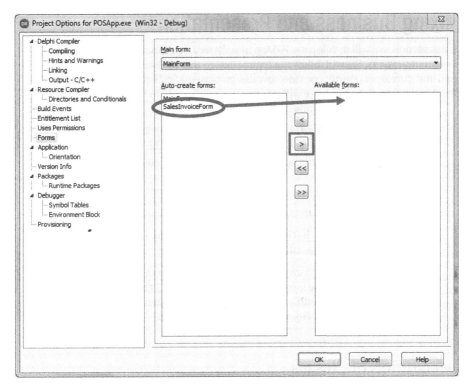

Figure 2-7. *The form options for the POSApp project*

Switch to the `MainScreenForm.pas` unit. We will now add code to the `ButtonInvoice` in order to open the `InvoiceForm`. Select the `ButtonInvoice`, click on the `OnClick` event (or click on the button itself), and add the following code. You also need to make sure that you declare the `InvoiceForm` in the unit's `uses` clause.

```
uses
  ..., InvoiceForm;

procedure TMainForm.ButtonInvoiceClick(Sender: TObject);
var
  tmpInvoiceForm: TSalesInvoiceForm;
begin
  tmpInvoiceForm:=TSalesInvoiceForm.Create(self);
  tmpInvoiceForm.ShowModal;
end;
```

Compile and run the application. Click on the Issue Invoice button. You should now be able to see the invoice form.

Mixing Business and Presentation

In this section, we will develop the POSApp in such way that mixes business logic and presentation layers. We will follow the typical design that evolves when RAD tools are used and developers do not consider any design patterns (called monolithic design). Then, in the rest of the book, we will refactor this application to the MVVM pattern.

We need the following entities (classes) for POSApp:

- *TCustomer*: A class that represents a customer and keeps track of the name of the customer, the current outstanding balance, the discount rate the customer is eligible for, and the ID of the customer.

- *TItem*: A class that holds an item to be sold. It has a field for the description of the item, its price, and ID number.

- *TInvoice*: A class that represents an invoice. It has an ID field and a sequence number (the invoice no.).

- *TInvoiceItem*: Each invoice includes items for a specific transaction. This class keeps the following data for each invoice item: ID (rank number), itemID, invoiceID (the invoice the item belongs to), the price per unit item, and the quantity of the item.

Declaration of Classes

To keep things organized in the code, we will keep all the declarations of the classes in one unit. Add a new unit to the project (you can use the Add New ➤ Unit option from the popup menu, as shown in Figure 2-5) and save it as Declarations.pas. Then, add the following code to the unit.

```
unit Declarations;

interface

type
  TCustomer = class
  private
    fID: Integer;
    fName: string;
    fDiscountRate: Double;
    fBalance: Currency;
  public
    property ID: integer read fID write fID;
    property Name: string read fName write fName;
    property DiscountRate: double read fDiscountRate write fDiscountRate;
    property Balance: Currency read fBalance write fBalance;
  end;
```

```
  TItem = class
  private
    fID: Integer;
    fDescription: string;
    fPrice: Currency;
  public
    property ID: integer read fID write fID;
    property Description: string read fDescription write fDescription;
    property Price: Currency read fPrice write fPrice;
  end;

  TInvoice = class
  private
    fID: integer;
    fNumber: integer;
    fCustomerID: integer;
  public
    property ID: Integer read fID write fID;
    property Number: Integer read fNumber write fNumber;
    property CustomerID: Integer read fCustomerID write fCustomerID;
  end;

TInvoiceItem = class
  private
    fID: integer;
    fInvoiceID: integer;
    fItemID: integer;
    fUnitPrice: Currency;
    fQuantity: integer;
  public
    property ID: integer read fID write fID;
    property InvoiceID: integer read fInvoiceID write fInvoiceID;
    property ItemID: integer read fItemID write fItemID;
    property UnitPrice: Currency read fUnitPrice write fUnitPrice;
    property Quantity: Integer read fQuantity write fQuantity;
  end;

implementation

end.
```

The Database Unit

Create a new unit and save it as Database.pas. This unit represents the persistent medium of your application. In a real-life application, you are most likely to use local and/or remote databases but, in this case, we will use hard-coded data. We will generate customer records, balances, and discount rates manually in the Create event of the class.

23

Now we will create a TDatabase class to simulate the "persistent" data. In the interface section of the Database.pas unit, add the following code:

```
uses Declarations, System.Generics.Collections;

type
  TDatabase = class
  private
    fCustomers: TObjectList<TCustomer>;
    fItems: TObjectList<TItem>;
  public
    constructor Create;
    destructor Destroy; override;
  end;
```

The class we created does not offer a way to expose the private fields. At this stage, we will use the constructor to simulate the creation of records in a "persistent" medium, as described. Later in this chapter, we will develop the class further to provide access to the private fields according to our needs.

The code in the implementation section for the constructor and deconstructor is as follows. As you can see, we create a set of customers and items to resemble data retrieved from dynamic storage.

```
{ TDatabase }

constructor TDatabase.Create;
var
  tmpCustomer: TCustomer;
  tmpItem: TItem;
begin
  inherited;

  fCustomers:=TObjectList<TCustomer>.Create;

  //Create mock customers
  tmpCustomer:=TCustomer.Create;
  tmpCustomer.ID:=1;
  tmpCustomer.Name:='John';
  tmpCustomer.DiscountRate:=12.50;
  tmpCustomer.Balance:=-Random(5000);
  fCustomers.Add(tmpCustomer);

  tmpCustomer:=TCustomer.Create;
  tmpCustomer.ID:=2;
  tmpCustomer.Name:='Alex';
  tmpCustomer.DiscountRate:=23.00;
  tmpCustomer.Balance:=-Random(2780);
  fCustomers.Add(tmpCustomer);
```

```
  tmpCustomer:=TCustomer.Create;
  tmpCustomer.ID:=3;
  tmpCustomer.Name:='Peter';
  tmpCustomer.DiscountRate:=0.0;
  tmpCustomer.Balance:=-Random(9000);
  fCustomers.Add(tmpCustomer);

  tmpCustomer:=TCustomer.Create;
  tmpCustomer.ID:=4;
  tmpCustomer.Name:='Retail Customer';
  tmpCustomer.DiscountRate:=0.0;
  tmpCustomer.Balance:=0.0;
  fCustomers.Add(tmpCustomer);

  fItems:=TObjectList<TItem>.Create;
  //Create mock items to sell
  tmpItem:=TItem.Create;
  tmpItem.ID:=100;
  tmpItem.Description:='T-shirt';
  tmpItem.Price:=13.55;
  fItems.Add(tmpItem);

  tmpItem:=TItem.Create;
  tmpItem.ID:=200;
  tmpItem.Description:='Trousers';
  tmpItem.Price:=23.45;
  fItems.Add(tmpItem);

  tmpItem:=TItem.Create;
  tmpItem.ID:=300;
  tmpItem.Description:='Coat';
  tmpItem.Price:=64.00;
  fItems.Add(tmpItem);

  tmpItem:=TItem.Create;
  tmpItem.ID:=400;
  tmpItem.Description:='Shirt';
  tmpItem.Price:=28.00;
  fItems.Add(tmpItem);
end;

destructor TDatabase.Destroy;
begin
  fCustomers.Free;
  fItems.Free;
  inherited;
end;
```

Total Sales

The main screen of POSApp has a field that shows the total sales figure. If we want to implement this, we need to have a way to store the sales that we generate every time we issue an invoice. As before, in real-life applications, this figure is typically stored in a database or calculated on-the-fly by accessing a database. Here, I use a normal text file to keep track of the invoice amounts. This is, admittedly, a naïve and poor approach, but it will serve our purposes. Delphi provides a very handy way to meet our needs, by providing the TIniFile class.

■ **Note** If you are not familiar with the TIniFile class in Delphi, check out this resource (DocWiki, 2016a).

In the TDatabase class, add one private field to hold the path and the filename of the file and two procedures to retrieve (GetTotalSales) the total amount and save (SaveCurrentSales) each invoice's sales amount. You also need to update the constructor and the uses clause in the implementation section.

```
interface
type
  TDatabase = class                    These are the
  private
  const                                sections in the INI
    SalesSection = 'Sales';
    SalesTotal = 'Total Sales';
  var
    fCustomers: TObjectList<TCustomer>;    This holds the path and
    fItems: TObjectList<TItem>;
    fFullFileName: string;                 filename of the ini file
  public
    ...
    function GetTotalSales: Currency;
    procedure SaveCurrentSales(const currentSales: Currency);
    ...
  end;

implementation

uses
  System.IniFiles, System.SysUtils, System.IOUtils;

...

constructor TDatabase.Create;
var                                         This contructs the
  ...
begin                                       full path
  inherited;
  fFullFileName:=TPath.Combine(ExtractFilePath(ParamStr(0)), 'POSApp.data');
  ...
end;
```

```
function TDatabase.GetTotalSales: Currency;
var
  tmpINIFile: TIniFile;
  amount: Currency;
begin
  amount:=0.00;
  tmpINIFile:=TIniFile.Create(fFullFileName);
  try
    amount:=tmpINIFile.ReadFloat(SalesSection,SalesTotal,0.00);
  finally
    tmpINIFile.Free;
    result:=amount;
  end;
end;

procedure TDatabase.SaveCurrentSales(const currentSales: Currency);
var
  tmpINIFile: TIniFile;
begin
  tmpINIFile:=TIniFile.Create(fFullFileName);
  try

    tmpINIFile.WriteFloat(SalesSection,SalesTotal,
GetTotalSales+currentSales);
  finally
    tmpINIFile.Free;
  end;
end;
```

▪ **Note**   When I present code, I attempt to use good programming practices whenever the scope justifies the complexity. In the previous code, I used the `try...finally` block to make sure the INI object is properly managed even if an exception is thrown. You can learn more about how to manage exceptions in this link (DocWiki, 2016b).

We initialize the value of `fFullFileName` to point to the folder of the executable file. If your target is set to Win32 and the build configuration is set to Debug, the `POSApp.data` file will be created in:

```
{the path you store the project files}\Win32\Debug
```

`GetTotalSales` opens the INI file and loads the Total Sales value from the Sales section of the file. `SaveCurrentSales` takes the amount of the current invoice and adds it to the saved sales figure.

The Main Form

The last thing we need to implement is a way for the main screen to update the total amount of sales. Return to the MainScreenForm unit and create a private procedure entitled UpdateTotalSales.

```
uses
  ..., Database;

type
  TMainForm = class(TForm)
    ...
    procedure FormCreate(Sender: TObject);
    procedure FormDestroy(Sender: TObject);
  private
    procedure UpdateTotalSales;
  public
    { Public declarations }
  end;
```

Enter the following code in the OnCreate event and, then, develop UpdateTotalSales (click anywhere in the class declaration and press Ctrl+Shift+C. Delphi will automatically create the skeleton of the procedure).

```
procedure TMainForm.FormCreate(Sender: TObject);
begin
  UpdateTotalSales;
end;

procedure TMainForm.UpdateTotalSales;
var
  tmpSales: Currency;
  tmpDatabase: TDatabase;
begin
  tmpSales:=0.00;

  tmpDatabase:=TDatabase.Create;
  try
    tmpSales:=tmpDatabase.GetTotalSales;
  finally
    tmpDatabase.Free;
  end;
```

```
  LabelTotalSalesFigure.Text:=Format('%10.2f',[tmpSales]);
end;
```

POSApp updates the total sales label when the form is created. You'll also want this to happen when you complete an invoice in the InvoiceForm screen. You do this by adding a call to UpdateTotalSales in the OnClick event of the ButtonInvoice.

```
procedure TMainForm.ButtonInvoiceClick(Sender: TObject);
var
  ...
begin
  ...
  UpdateTotalSales;
end;
```

The Sales Invoice Form

Let's move to the InvoiceForm unit. Open the form and go to the Code panel. In order to implement the invoice functionality, we need a number of variables to keep track of the invoice. The following fields are introduced in the private section of the TSalesInvoiceForm. You also need to update the uses part of the unit.

```
uses
  ..., Database, Declarations, System.Generics.Collections;

type
  TSalesInvoiceForm = class(TForm)
    ...
  private
    fDatabase: TDatabase;          ← This holds a reference to the database
    fInvoice: TInvoice;            ← This is the invoice class
    fCurrentCustomer:TCustomer;    ← This is the customer's class
    fCurrentInvoiceItems: TObjectList<TInvoiceItem>; ← The items of the
                                                       invoice
    fCurrentInvoiceBalance: Currency; ← The current balance of the
  public                              invoice
    { Public declarations }
  end;
```

We need to initialize the classes and free them when the form closes. Add the following code to the OnCreate and OnDestroy events of the form.

```
procedure TSalesInvoiceForm.FormCreate(Sender: TObject);
begin
  fDatabase:=TDatabase.Create;
  fInvoice:=TInvoice.Create;     We give an ID number to the invoice
  fInvoice.ID:=1; ◄─────────────────────
  fInvoice.Number:=Random(3000); ◄───────────── We give a random invoice Nr.
  fCurrentInvoiceItems:=TObjectList<TInvoiceItem>.Create;
end;

procedure TSalesInvoiceForm.FormDestroy(Sender: TObject);
begin
  fInvoice.Free;
  fCurrentInvoiceItems.Free;
  fDatabase.Free;
end;
```

An inspection of the InvoiceForm shows that there is a workflow that defines which fields the user can access and when. For example, there is no point to add items to an invoice before the user selects a customer (even a generic anonymous retail customer) or to apply a discount. This means that we need an initial setup of the properties of the components. Once the form is created, we can set up the interface. Add the following procedure to the private section of the form and complete the code.

```
type
  TSalesInvoiceForm = class(TForm)
    ...
  private
    ...
    procedure SetupGUI;
  public
    { Public declarations }
  end;

procedure TSalesInvoiceForm.SetupGUI;
var
  tmpCustomerList: TObjectList<TCustomer>;
  tmpCustomer: TCustomer;
  tmpItemsList: TObjectList<TItem>;
  tmpItem: TItem;
begin
  LabelTitle.Text:='Sales Invoice #'+fInvoice.Number.ToString;
  PopupBoxCustomer.Clear;
  PopupBoxItems.Clear;
  GroupBoxInvoiceItems.Enabled:=false;
  GroupBoxBalance.Enabled:=false;
  ButtonPrintInvoice.Enabled:=false;
  LabelInvoiceBalance.Text:=Format('%-n',[0.00]);

  //Load data from "database"
  tmpCustomerList:=fDatabase.GetCustomerList;      We get the customers
  if Assigned(tmpCustomerList) then                from the database
  begin
    for tmpCustomer in tmpCustomerList  do
      if Assigned(tmpCustomer) then
        PopupBoxCustomer.Items.Add(tmpCustomer.Name);
  end;
  PopupBoxCustomer.ItemIndex:=-1;

  tmpItemsList:=fDatabase.GetItems;                We get the items we can
  if Assigned(tmpItemsList) then                   sell from the database
  begin
    for tmpItem in tmpItemsList do
      if Assigned(tmpItem) then
        PopupBoxItems.Items.Add(tmpItem.Description);
  end;
  PopupBoxItems.ItemIndex:=-1;

  EditQuantity.Text:='1';

  StringGridItems.RowCount:=0;

  AniIndicatorProgress.Visible:=false;
  LabelPrinting.Visible:=false;
  end;
```

First, we set up the labels, clear the popup boxes, and disable the group boxes. Then we load the customer list (GetCustomerList) and the items (GetItems) from the database and update the relevant popup boxes.

Retrieving Data

Switch back to the Database unit and add the following functions to the TDatabase class. Now, we will add methods to expose the private fields we declared earlier.

```
interface
 ...

type
  TDatabase = class
  private
    ...
  public
    ...
    function GetCustomerList: TObjectList<TCustomer>;
    function GetItems: TObjectList<TItem>;
    ...
  end;

implementation

...

function TDatabase.GetCustomerList: TObjectList<TCustomer>;
begin
  result:=fCustomers;
end;

function TDatabase.GeTItems: TObjectList<TItem>;
begin
  result:=fItems;
end;
```

These functions simply return the lists from the TDatabase class. Back to InvoiceForm, the SetupGUI procedure cleans the edit field and the string grid and makes the animated progress indicator and the label at the bottom invisible. If you execute POSApp and open an invoice, you should be able to select a customer from the popup box.

The last thing that is left to do in the Customer Detail group box is to update the Discount Rate and the Outstanding Balance fields that appear when the user selects a customer name in the popup box. In the Database unit, the customer list is stored as an object list of TCustomer classes. When the user makes a selection in the popup box for the customers, we only have the name of the customer. Therefore, we need a way to get the TCustomer class from the name. Go back to the Database unit and add the following function.

```
interface

...

type
  TDatabase = class
  private
    ...
  public
    ...
    function GetCustomerFromName(const nameStr: string): TCustomer;
    ...
  end;

implementation

function TDatabase.GetCustomerFromName(const nameStr: string): TCustomer;
var
  tmpCustomer: TCustomer;
begin
  if not Assigned(fCustomers) then Exit;
  result:=nil;
  for tmpCustomer in fCustomers do
  begin
    if tmpCustomer.Name=nameStr then
    begin
      result:=tmpCustomer;
      exit;
    end;
  end;
end;
```

Now we have a way to retrieve the TCustomer class from the customer name. Switch to the InvoiceForm unit, click on the OnChange event of the PopupBoxCustomer component, and add the following code:

```
interface
...

type
  TSalesInvoiceForm = class(TForm)
    ...
    procedure PopupBoxCustomerChange(Sender: TObject);
  private
    ...
  end;
...

implementation

...


procedure TSalesInvoiceForm.PopupBoxCustomerChange(Sender: TObject);
var
 tmpCustomer: TCustomer;
begin
   if not Assigned(fDatabase) then Exit;

   tmpCustomer:=fDatabase.GetCustomerFromName(PopupBoxCustomer.Text);
   if Assigned(tmpCustomer) then
   begin
     LabelDiscountRateFigure.Text:=
           Format('%5.2f',[tmpCustomer.DiscountRate])+'%';
     LabelTotalBalanceBig.Text:=Format('%-n',[tmpCustomer.Balance]);
     if tmpCustomer.Balance>=0 then
       LabelTotalBalanceBig.FontColor:=TAlphaColorRec.Green
     else
       LabelTotalBalanceBig.FontColor:=TAlphaColorRec.Red;
     fCurrentCustomer:=tmpCustomer;
     fCurrentInvoiceItems.Clear;

     GroupBoxInvoiceItems.Enabled:=true;
     GroupBoxBalance.Enabled:=true;
     CheckBoxDiscount.IsChecked:=false;

     StringGridItems.RowCount:=0;
     LabelInvoiceBalance.Text:=Format('%-n',[0.00]);
     LabelRunningBalance.Text:=Format('%-n',[0.00]);
     LabelTotalBalance.Text:=Format('%-n', [0.00]);

     PopupBoxItems.ItemIndex:=-1;
   end;
end;
```

This is not necessary, as in this case, we control the fDatabase object, but it is good practice

Here we get the customer class

34

The code is straightforward; after retrieving the appropriate TCustomer class, it updates the user interface accordingly and enables the relevant parts. The code also cleans the string grid when the customer popup menu changes.

Similar to the need we had earlier to retrieve the customer class from the name, we need to be able to get the item's class from its description. In the Database unit, add the following method.

```
type
  TDatabase = class
  private
    ...
  public
    ...
    function GetItemFromDescription(const desc: string): TItem;
    ...
  end;
...

implementation
...

function TDatabase.GetItemFromDescription(const desc: string): TItem;
var
  tmpItem: TItem;
begin
  result:=nil;
  if not Assigned(fItems) then Exit;
  for tmpItem in fItems do
  begin
    if tmpItem.Description=desc then
    begin
      result:=tmpItem;
      exit;
    end;
  end;
end;
```

Updating the Form

The PopupBoxItems menu is enabled when the user selects a customer. We will add the code to update the list with the selected item and the quantity. Click on the Add Item button and add the following code.

```
interface
...

type
  TSalesInvoiceForm = class(TForm)
    ...
    procedure ButtonAddItemClick(Sender: TObject);
  private
    ...
  public
    { Public declarations }
  end;

...

implementation
...

procedure TSalesInvoiceForm.ButtonAddItemClick(Sender: TObject);
var
  tmpInvoiceItem: TInvoiceItem;
  tmpItem: TItem;
begin
  if trim(PopupBoxItems.Text)='' then
  begin
    ShowMessage('Please choose an item');
    PopupBoxItems.SetFocus;
    Exit;
  end;

  if trim(EditQuantity.Text)='' then
  begin
    ShowMessage('Please enter quantity');
    EditQuantity.SetFocus;
    Exit;
  end;

  if EditQuantity.Text.ToInteger<=0 then
  begin
    ShowMessage('The quantity must be positive number');
    EditQuantity.SelectAll;
    EditQuantity.SetFocus;
  end;

  tmpInvoiceItem:=TInvoiceItem.Create;
  tmpInvoiceItem.ID:=StringGridItems.RowCount+1;
  tmpInvoiceItem.InvoiceID:=fInvoice.ID;
  tmpInvoiceItem.Quantity:=EditQuantity.Text.ToInteger;
```

```
tmpItem:=fDatabase.GetItemFromDescription(PopupBoxItems.Text);
  if not Assigned(tmpItem) then Exit;
```
The code refers to items based on their
```
  tmpInvoiceItem.ItemID:=tmpItem.ID;
  tmpInvoiceItem.UnitPrice:=tmpItem.Price;
```
IDs, as you would if you had a real-life database design
```
  fCurrentInvoiceItems.Add(tmpInvoiceItem);
```
This method shows the items
```
UpdateInvoiceGrid;
```
in the StringGrid
```
 UpdateBalance;
end;
```
This method updates the total balance of the invoice.

The method applies a number of validation checks and adds the new invoice item to the fCurrentInvoiceItems list. We update the user interface (the string grid and the label with the total invoice amount) using the two procedures at the end of the previous method. You can develop the two procedures with the following code.

```
interface
...

type
  TSalesInvoiceForm = class(TForm)
    ...
  private
    ...
    procedure UpdateBalance;
    procedure UpdateInvoiceGrid;
  public
    { Public declarations }
  end;

...

implementation

...

procedure TSalesInvoiceForm.UpdateBalance;
var
  RunningBalance,
  discount: Currency;
  i: integer;
begin
  RunningBalance:=0.00;
  discount:=0.00;
  fCurrentInvoiceBalance:=0.00;
```

```
for i := 0 to StringGridItems.RowCount-1 do
  RunningBalance:=RunningBalance+StringGridItems.Cells[3,i].ToDouble;
LabelRunningBalance.Text:=Format('%10.2f',[RunningBalance]);
if CheckBoxDiscount.IsChecked then          ◀──────────────
  discount:=RunningBalance*fCurrentCustomer.DiscountRate/100;
LabelDiscount.Text:=Format('%10.2f',[-discount]);
RunningBalance:=RunningBalance - discount;
fCurrentInvoiceBalance:=RunningBalance;

LabelTotalBalance.Text:=Format('%10.2f',[runningBalance]);
LabelInvoiceBalance.Text:=Format('%10.2f',[runningBalance]);

  ButtonPrintInvoice.Enabled:=StringGridItems.RowCount > 0;
end;

procedure TSalesInvoiceForm.UpdateInvoiceGrid;
var
  tmpInvoiceItem: TInvoiceItem;
  tmpItem: TItem;
begin
  StringGridItems.RowCount:=0;
  for tmpInvoiceItem in fCurrentInvoiceItems do
  begin
    tmpItem:=fDatabase.GetItemFromID(tmpInvoiceItem.ItemID);
    if Assigned(tmpItem) then
    begin
      StringGridItems.RowCount := StringGridItems.RowCount + 1;
      StringGridItems.Cells[0, StringGridItems.RowCount - 1] :=
tmpItem.Description;
      StringGridItems.Cells[1, StringGridItems.RowCount - 1] :=
tmpInvoiceItem.Quantity.ToString;
      StringGridItems.Cells[2, StringGridItems.RowCount - 1] :=
format('%10.2f', [tmpInvoiceItem.UnitPrice]);
      StringGridItems.Cells[3, StringGridItems.RowCount - 1] :=
format('%10.2f', [tmpInvoiceItem.Quantity * tmpInvoiceItem.UnitPrice]);
      StringGridItems.Cells[4, StringGridItems.RowCount - 1] :=
tmpInvoiceItem.ID.ToString;
    end;
  end;
  PopupMenuItems.Items[0].Enabled := StringGridItems.RowCount > 0;
end;
```

Calculate the discount rate

This gets the item class from the item's ID

We need to add the code for the GetItemFromID procedure (Database unit), which appears in UpdateInvoiceGrid, as indicated previously.

```
type
  TDatabase = class
  private
    ...
  public
    ...
```

```
    function GetItemFromID(const id: Integer): TItem;
      ...
  end;
...

implementation
...

function TDatabase.GetItemFromID(const id: Integer): TItem;
var
  tmpItem: TItem;
begin
  result:=nil;
  if not Assigned(fItems) then Exit;
  for tmpItem in fItems do
  begin
    if tmpItem.ID=id then
    begin
      result:=tmpItem;
      exit;
    end;
  end;
end;
```

Run the application. You should be able to add items in the invoice and then view the updated invoice amount.

There are a few things left. In the InvoiceForm, select the PopupMenuItems popup menu component, open the Items Editor, and open a TMenuItem labeled Delete Entry. Select the menu item you created and implement the OnClick event.

```
interface
...

type
  TSalesInvoiceForm = class(TForm)
    ...
    procedure MenuItemDeleteItemClick(Sender: TObject);
  private
    ...
  public
    { Public declarations }
  end;

...

implementation

...
```

```
procedure TSalesInvoiceForm.MenuItemDeleteItemClick(Sender: TObject);
var
  tmpInvoiceItem: TInvoiceItem;
begin
  if (StringGridItems.Selected>=0) and
    (StringGridItems.Selected<=StringGridItems.RowCount-1) then
  begin
    for tmpInvoiceItem in fCurrentInvoiceItems do
      if tmpInvoiceItem.ID=
        StringGridItems.Cells[4,StringGridItems.Selected].ToInteger then
        begin
          fCurrentInvoiceItems.RemoveItem(tmpInvoiceItem, TDirection.
FromBeginning);
          break;
        end;
  end;
  UpdateInvoiceGrid;
  UpdateBalance;
end;
```

Select the CheckBoxDiscount check box and write the OnChange event to update the discounted amount, as you have already considered the discount in UpdateBalance.

```
interface
...

type
  TSalesInvoiceForm = class(TForm)
    ...
    procedure CheckBoxDiscountChange(Sender: TObject);
  private
    ...
  public
    { Public declarations }
  end;

...

implementation

...
procedure TSalesInvoiceForm.CheckBoxDiscountChange(Sender: TObject);
begin
  UpdateBalance;
end;
```

When the user is ready to issue an invoice, they select the Print Invoice button. If they want to cancel it, they simply select Cancel. The code behind the OnClick events of the two buttons looks like this:

```
interface
...

type
  TSalesInvoiceForm = class(TForm)
    ...
    procedure ButtonPrintInvoiceClick(Sender: TObject);
    procedure ButtonCancelClick(Sender: TObject);
  private
    ...
  public
    { Public declarations }
  end;

...

implementation

...
procedure TSalesInvoiceForm.ButtonPrintInvoiceClick(Sender: TObject);
begin
  if fCurrentInvoiceItems.Count>0 then
  begin
    AniIndicatorProgress.Visible:=true;
    LabelPrinting.Visible:=true;
    ShowMessage('Invoice Printed');
    if Assigned(fDatabase) then
      fDatabase.SaveCurrentSales(fCurrentInvoiceBalance);
    self.Close;
  end;
end;

procedure TSalesInvoiceForm.ButtonCancelClick(Sender: TObject);
begin
  self.Close;
end;
```

Here we save the invoice Amount

The Cancel button simply closes the form and the Print Invoice button shows a message and stores the invoice amount to our "database".

At this point, we have completed the POSApp. As you see, this implementation provides the code that accesses our database and performs calculations (the business logic) next to the code that updates the user interface (the presentation). If you want to replace the form with another one, you need to spend a lot of time and effort developing all the procedures of the new form. In fact, it does not have to be a completely new form. You can face the same difficulty if you replace components in the form.

For example, in the SalesInvoiceForm unit, we run a few calculations in several places and update the GUI elements accordingly. If, at some point, we want to show the discount rate in a pie chart or add a track bar to allow users to define the quantities to the invoice items, we would need to visit all those places in the form and amend the code that retrieves or shows this information. These kinds of complications, which are prone to errors and bugs, are minimized and even avoided with the MVVM approach.

Summary

In this chapter, we created the POSApp application with code that mixes business logic, presentation, and view states. In other words, at this stage, POSApp is a tightly coupled application.

By the end of this book, we will have a version of the application that allows us to replace the view or the graphical elements with minimal effort. In the next chapter, we will visit the foundations of a MVVM architecture in terms of coding and we develop a methodology that allows us to convert POSApp to an MVVM application.

References

Begel, A. and Nagappan, N., 2007. "Usage and Perceptions of Agile Software Development in an Industrial Context: An Exploratory Study," *First International Symposium on Empirical Software Engineering and Measurement (ESEM 2007)*, pp.255-264.

DocWiki, E., 2016a. "Using TIniFile and TMemIniFile," available at http://docwiki. embarcadero.com/RADStudio/Seattle/en/Using_TIniFile_and_TMemIniFile [Accessed 17/03/2016].

DocWiki, E., 2016b. "Writing Exception Handlers," available at http://docwiki. embarcadero.com/RADStudio/Seattle/en/Writing_Exception_Handlers [Accessed 17/03/2016].

Gerber, A., Van Der Merwe, A., and Alberts, R., 2007. "Practical Implications of Rapid Development Methodologies".

CHAPTER 3

■ ■ ■

MVVM as Design Philosophy

In the previous chapter, we developed the POSApp using an all-in-one approach. We will start converting the application to MVVM by looking at the view and considering which functions should stay with it and which functionality will be delivered by the ViewModel and the Model. I start exploring the MVVM pattern from the View, but this is not necessary; you can begin your design from the Model or the ViewModel. Here, we will use the View as a starting point, as it is easier to demonstrate a way of approaching the design of an application in the MVVM domain.

■ **Note** The more familiar you become with the MVVM pattern, the easier it becomes to work out the ViewModel first. ViewModels work as a bridge between the Model and the View and allow different teams in bigger projects to work separately and in parallel without losing focus. For example, you may have a group of developers working on the models and the ViewModels of your application and a designer crafting the user interface and experience without the need for the latter to wait until your developers complete an important part of the application.

The View of the MainScreen

The main screen of POSApp is pretty simple. It has a number of static labels, a button that opens the invoice form, and one label that shows the updated sales figure. The most obvious element that deserves its place in a ViewModel or in a Model is the total sales figure. We map the visualization of the total sales figure to a property in the ViewModel, which in turn receives its value from the Model itself via a function. Figure 3-1 shows this relationship. The aim is to create a view that is as *thin* as possible and empty from elements that define the *view logic* and *view state*. In this sense, we treat the static labels' text and the button's text as parameterized (for example, in an application that requires translations) and we map them to separate fields and properties.

© John Kouraklis 2016
J. Kouraklis, *MVVM in Delphi*, DOI 10.1007/978-1-4842-2214-0_3

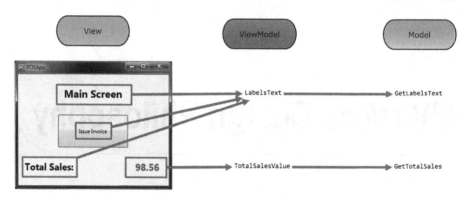

Figure 3-1. *Main screen in an MVVM approach*

Follow the next steps:

1. Create a new folder to store the new version of POSApp. Call it POSAppMVVM. Within this folder, create three new folders called Models, ViewModels, and Views.

2. Create a new multi-device application (Blank application) in Delphi, save the new unit as Views.MainForm in the Views folder, save the project as POSAppMVVM in the POSAppMVVM folder, and then save the project group in the POSAppMVVM folder as POSAppMVVMProjectGroup.

3. Go to the Design tab of the MainForm and add the components of the form as you did in the previous chapter (refer back to Figure 2-4). This time, use dummy text for the labels (we will retrieve the actual values from the ViewModel).

■ **Tip** In the book's code, you will find the files (View.ModelForm.fmx and View. ModelForm.pas) of an empty version of the MainForm for your convenience. They are located in the Thin Forms folder. You can import them in an empty project (using the menu in Figure 2-5 and the Add option) instead of creating the components from scratch.

The Designer of the form and the Project Manager of your IDE environment should look very similar to Figure 3-2. Note that the form file in the right sidebar is located in the Views folder. This will help us keep the files organized while we are developing the project.

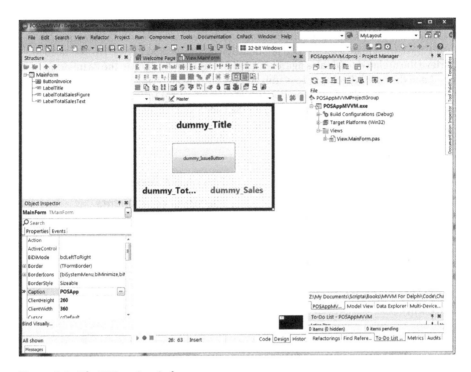

Figure 3-2. *The IDE main window*

The Model of the MainScreen

The model of the MainForm provides two functions, as discussed (see Figure 3-1). Remember that the model is now responsible for accessing any data sources and performing all the required manipulations to supply data to the ViewModel.

1. Create a new unit and save it as `Model.Main.pas` in the `Models` folder.

2. You need the `Declarations.pas` and `Database.pas` units from the first version of `POSApp`. Copy the original files and paste them into the `Models` folder. Then, you can add the units to the project. For consistency, you can rename the files to `Model.Declarations` and `Model.Database`, but this is not necessary. If you decide to rename the files, you need to change the unit declarations too.

3. Create a new unit and save it as `Model.Main.pas`.

According to the plan, we need to be able to retrieve the labels of the components. We could create separate functions for each one, but we will follow a simpler apprach instead. We will create a record and populate it with the desired values. We also need to retrieve the updated total sales figures, a job that was initially done in the MainForm.

Load the Model.Declarations unit and declare the following record. Title field keeps the caption of the LabelTitle component; IssueButtonCaption refers to the text of ButtonInvoice; and TotalSalesText is for the LabelTotalSales element.

```
unit Model.Declarations;

interface
...
```

This record keeps the text of the visual components

```
  TMainFormLabelsText = record   ◄──────────────
    Title,
    IssueButtonCaption,
    TotalSalesText: string;
  end;

implementation
...

end.
```

Switch to the Model.Main unit and add the following code. You have to declare the Model.Declarations, Model.Database, and System.SysUtils units in the uses clauses.

You can now add the GetTotalSales, which is the last function of this unit. This is a simple reference to the appropriate function in the Model.Database unit.

```
unit Model.Main;

interface

uses Model.Declarations, Model.Database;

type
  TMainModel = class
  private
    fMainFormLabelsText: TMainFormLabelsText;
    fDatabase: TDatabase;
  public
    function GetMainFormLabelsText: TMainFormLabelsText;
    constructor Create;
    destructor Destroy; override;
  end;

implementation

uses
  System.SysUtils;

{ TMainModel }

constructor TMainModel.Create;
begin
  fDatabase:=TDatabase.Create;
end;

destructor TMainModel.Destroy;
begin
  fDatabase.Free;
  inherited;
end;

function TMainModel.GetMainFormLabelsText: TMainFormLabelsText;
begin
  fMainFormLabelsText.Title:='Main Screen';
  fMainFormLabelsText.IssueButtonCaption:='Issue Invoice';
  fMainFormLabelsText.TotalSalesText:='Total Sales:';
  result:=fMainFormLabelsText;
end;

end;
```

Reference to the label captions record

Reference to the database

```
interface
...

type
  TMainModel = class
  private
    ...
  public
    ...
    function GetTotalSales: Currency;
    ...
  end;

implementation
...

function TMainModel.GetTotalSales: Currency;
begin
  result:=fDatabase.GetTotalSales;
end;

end.
```

Note the use of a data access layer from within the model

The ViewModel of the MainScreen

As mentioned in Chapter 1, the ViewModel has direct access to the Model. Create a new unit and save it as ViewModel.Main.pas in the ViewModels folder. We will build the code that receives data from the model and transforms it to information that makes sense to the view (view logic/view state).

```
unit ViewModel.Main;

interface

uses Model.Main, Model.Declarations;

type
  TMainViewModel = class                    Reference to the Model
  private
    fModel: TMainModel;
    fLabelsText: TMainFormLabelsText;            Hold the values
    fTotalSalesValue: Currency;                  retrieved from the
    procedure SetModel (const newModel: TMainModel);   Model
    function GetLabelsText: TMainFormLabelsText;
  public
    property Model: TMainModel read fModel write SetModel;
    property LabelsText: TMainFormLabelsText read GetlabelsText;
    function GetTotalSalesValue: string;
    destructor Destroy; override;           Notice that this returns a
  end;                                      string type and not a
                                            currency type
implementation

uses
  System.SysUtils;

{ TMainViewModel }


function TMainViewModel.GetLabelsText: TMainFormLabelsText;
begin
  fLabelsText:=fModel.GetMainFormLabelsText;
  result:=fLabelsText;
end;

function TMainViewModel.GetTotalSalesValue: string;
begin
                                            Here you transform
                                            the sales value to a
  fTotalSalesValue:=fModel.GetTotalSales;   form useful to the
  result:=Format('%10.2f',[fTotalSalesValue]);   View
```

```
end;


procedure TMainViewModel.SetModel(const newModel: TMainModel);
begin
  fModel:=newModel;
end;


end.
```

We can move forward by linking the View to the ViewModel. Open the View.
MainForm form and include the following piece of code.

```
interface

uses
  ..., ViewModel.Main;

type
  TMainForm = class(TForm)
    ...
  private
    fViewModel: TMainViewModel; ◄───────────  Reference to the ViewModel
    procedure SetViewModel (const newViewModel: TMainViewModel);
    procedure UpdateLabels;
    procedure UpdateTotalSalesFigure;
  public
    property ViewModel: TMainViewModel read fViewModel write SetViewModel;
  end;


implementation

{$R *.fmx}

{ TMainForm }

procedure TMainForm.UpdateLabels;
begin
  LabelTitle.Text := fViewModel.LabelsText.Title;
  LabelTotalSalesText.Text := fViewModel.LabelsText.TotalSalesText;
  LabelTotalSalesFigure.Text := fViewModel.LabelsText.TotalSalesEmptyText;
end;


procedure TMainForm.UpdateTotalSalesFigure;
begin
  ButtonInvoice.Text := fViewModel.LabelsText.IssueButtonCaption;
end;
```

```
procedure TMainForm.SetViewModel(const newViewModel: TMainViewModel);
begin
  fViewModel:=newViewModel;
  UpdateLabels;
  UpdateTotalSalesFigure;
end;

end.
```

I have created two methods (UpdateLabels and UpdateTotalSalesFigure) to refresh the graphical elements. Although I could include the code in the SetViewModel directly, keeping the code separate serves several practical reasons, which will become apparent later in the next chapter.

Creating the Classes

If you compile and execute the project, you will only see the main form with the "dummy" labels. This is because we have not yet created the classes for the ViewModel and the Model. As mentioned in the first chapter, there are different approaches to this regarding which part of the MVVM structure should be created first. In this case, I will create the ViewModel and the Model after the creation of the View for simplicity as we are, already, in the MainForm. When we create the InvoiceForm, we will follow the other approach for demonstration purposes.

In MainForm, write this code in the OnCreate and OnDestroy events of the form.

```
unit View.MainForm;

interface

uses
  ..., ViewModel.Main;

type
  TMainForm = class(TForm)
    ...
    procedure FormCreate(Sender: TObject);
    procedure FormDestroy(Sender: TObject);
  private
    ...
    fViewModel: TViewModel;          Reference to the Model and View Model
  public
    ...
  end;

...

implementation

{$R *.fmx}
```

51

```
uses Model.Main;

{ TMainForm }

...
procedure TMainForm.FormCreate(Sender: TObject);
begin
  fmainModel:=TMainModel.Create;          This creates the Model
  fViewModel:=TMainViewModel.Create;        This creates the ViewModel
  fViewModel.Model:=mainModel;
  ViewModel:=fViewModel;                  This assigns the Model to the ViewModel
end;                                    This assigns the ViewModel to the View

procedure TMainForm.FormDestroy(Sender: TObject);
begin
  fMainModel.Free;
  fViewModel.Free;
end;

end.
```

How the Code Works

When the MainForm is created, the OnCreate event creates a new instance of TMainModel. Then, it creates a new ViewModel class (fViewModel) and assigns the Model to the ViewModel. Finally, the ViewModel is attached to the View and this completes the chain of M-VM-V (see Figure 3-3). One point you may notice in the code is that the mainModel variable is local to the FormCreate procedure and it survives even though the procedure ends. This is because we link mainModel to a variable that exists for the whole life of MainForm (fViewModel).

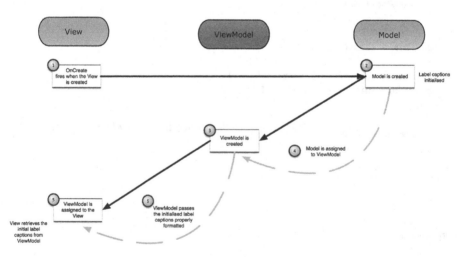

Figure 3-3. *Order of creation of classes in POSApp*

Creating the ViewModel and the Model Outside the Main Form

As you notice, we do all the job of creating the ViewModel and Model classes within the form. This receives some criticism from a number of MVVM fans on the basis that having all the elements in the View doesn't follow the MVVM principles and keeps the parts together in such way that testing becomes difficult. My view is that you observe this situation only when you set up the main form of the application. In regard to the argument about the separation of the elements, we have only created the classes in a procedure of the form and the form doesn't directly interact with the ViewModel or the Model and the communication follows the MVVM logic. Despite this, I will show you how to approach the creation of the ViewModel and the Model from outside the View.

1. Save `POSAppMVVMProjectGroup` and all its files in a different folder under a different name. The code that comes with the book uses the name `POSAppMVVMMainForm` for the folder and the project group.

2. Open `View.MainForm` and delete the `FormCreate` procedure.

3. Execute `POSApp`. You should see the main screen with the "dummy" labels and caption.

We are going to create the ViewModel and the Model classes before we create the main form.

1. Go to the Project ➤ Options ➤ Forms menu and move the `MainForm` from the Auto-Create Forms list to the Available Forms, as you did in the previous chapter (review Figure 2-7).

2. Select `POSAppMVVM.exe` or `POSAppMVVMMainForm.exe` if you are using the code from the book in the Project Manager panel. Open the source of the `.exe` file (choose View Source from the menu shown in Figure 2-5) or press Ctrl+V.

3. Enter the following lines of code:

```
program POSAppMVVM;

uses
  System.StartUpCopy,
  FMX.Forms,
  View.MainForm in 'Views\View.MainForm.pas' {MainForm},
  Model.Database in 'Models\Model.Database.pas',
  Model.Declarations in 'Models\Model.Declarations.pas',
  Model.Main in 'Models\Model.Main.pas',
  ViewModel.Main in 'ViewModels\ViewModel.Main.pas';

{$R *.res}

var
  mainModel: TMainModel;
  mainViewModel: TMainViewModel;

begin
  mainModel:=TMainModel.Create;
  mainViewModel:=TMainViewModel.Create;
  mainViewModel.Model:=mainModel;

  Application.Initialize;

  MainForm:=TMainForm.Create(Application);
  MainForm.ViewModel:=mainViewModel;

  Application.MainForm:=MainForm;
  MainForm.Show;
  Application.Run;
end.
```

We create the Model and the ViewModel and assign the Model to the ViewModel

The application is initialized

We create the form and assign the ViewModel

*We assign the MainForm to be the application's main form. This can **only** be done in FireMonkey; it doesn't work in VLC*

In a graphical presentation, the order of creation of the classes and the form is shown in Figure 3-4. The MainForm unit is very simple in this case and only holds the code to update the total figures label.

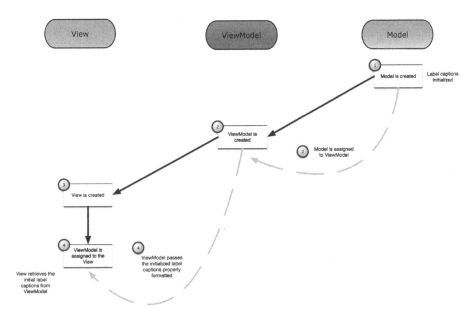

Figure 3-4. *Order of creation of classes outside the MainForm*

Notes About the Code

There are a few points to notice in the code we developed to implement the MVVM pattern for the MainForm.

1. Both Model.Main and View.MainForm are very light in the implementation.

2. ViewModel.Main is responsible for the way data is presented to the view. The GetLabelsText function deals with default values and the GetTotalSalesValue function formats the sales figure as retrieved from the model.

3. You may wonder why I get into the trouble to the trouble to retrieve the labels from the model instead of setting the captions directly in the form. Although it may look a small thing in this application, it is a great opportunity to challenge the way we see forms. Consider, for example, how you would change the design if you were asked to provide the ability to change the interface language at runtime. With this design, you would simply go to the model unit and add a few lines to the GetMainFormLabelsText function in order to get the translated text.

4. Following the previous point, the View now is totally detached from the text of the visual elements. This means that you can send the form files to an UI designer (with the lines for the class creation and retrieval of data commented) who is familiar with Delphi and they will do all the visual work for you. They can even rearrange the components as they feel best for the workflow. When you receive it back, what you have to do is uncomment all the lines in the code.

5. This example exposed the Model and ViewModel in the relevant classes by defining properties. I could, equally, use the SetModel (in ViewModel.Main) and the SetViewModel (in View.MainForm) to get the same result (both methods should be declared as public in that case). Properties allow the creation of fluent interfaces where you can directly write

   ```
   mainViewModel.Model:=mainModel;
   ```

   instead of calling the procedure

   ```
   mainViewMode.SetModel(mainModel);
   ```

   Other than this, there are no real benefits, so you can consider it a matter of personal preference.

6. What we achieve by declaring TMainViewModel and setting the View model and the Model to the form and the View model respectively is a high degree of isolation and, therefore, of reusability of the View model and the form classes. This is an example of what is called *dependency injection*. It allows programmers to modify at runtime any variables (dependencies) the classes require. For example, if you have the need, you can change the View Model of the main form without closing it or restarting the application.

7. If we wanted to control the color of the label in the main form, we would have to create a new field in the ViewModel and GetTotalSalesValue would set the value. The Model and the View would be ignorant of how we determined the color of the label separating, in this way, the *view logic* and the *view state* from the *view*.

How We Converted MainScreen

At this stage, we converted the MainScreen to follow the Model-ViewModel-View paradigm. Figure 3-5 explains the steps we followed.

1. We started with the MainScreen form (view). We recognized the visual elements and decided that we can not keep any code in the form that determines the content of the visual elements. Instead, the only code we host in the View just passes any values to the appropriate visual element (controls). Therefore, we needed to remove the part of the UpdateTotalSales method that decides on the *view state* and *view logic*. Initializing values is a *view state* and formatting values is *view logic*

2. The action in the first step implies that we need a "place" to format and initialize total sales. The obvious location for these activities is in the ViewModel. The ViewModel determines how the *view state* and *view logic* are implemented. Therefore, the ViewModel formats the TotalSalesValue and gives access to the view. We moved the code from the original UpdateTotalSales to the ViewModel under the method called TotalSalesValue.

3. What is left is the initialization and, subsequently, the updating of the values that are being passed to the view. This is the job of the Model. New, separate methods (GetLabelsText and GetTotalSales) appear in the Model.

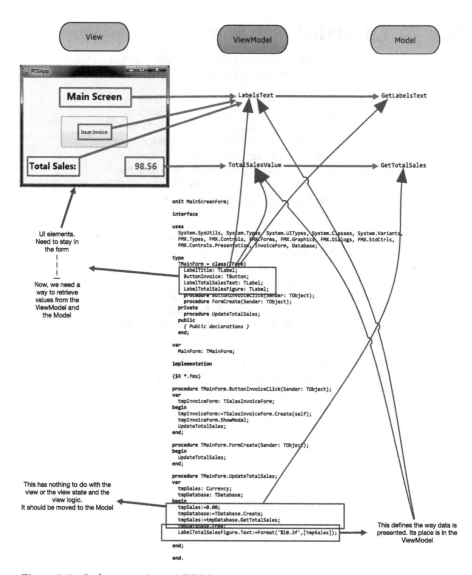

Figure 3-5. *Code conversion to MVVM*

Summary

In this chapter, we converted the first of the forms of the application in such way that follows the MVVM principles. Figure 3-5, along with the descriptions, epitomize the steps we followed to achieve this conversion. You can see them as the first part of a methodology that allows us to work on monolithic applications. Before we move to the second form of POSApp, we need to develop some tools in order to establish bi-directional access to the elements of MVVM. The next chapter deals with these tools.

CHAPTER 4

■ ■ ■

Two-Way Communication

Take a moment to revisit the code developed for POSApp so far. In particular, try to identify the way that communication is being delivered among the View, the ViewModel, and the Model. Then consider Figure 3-4 and the way the initial labels captions are retrieved. Based on this figure and the description of the layout of the MVVM model as presented in Chapter 1, we may notice that each one of the components communicate with the next in the layout in an one-way arrangement, as awareness of each element is limited. The View is aware of the ViewModel, but the ViewModel doesn't know anything about the View. Likewise, the ViewModel is aware of the Model, but not vice versa. This design has served us well in POSApp up to this point, as we simply wanted to get the values of the labels.

However, if we go back and run the version of POSApp developed in Chapter 2, we will notice that the Total Sales figure in the MainScreen is updated every time a new invoice is successfully issued. This implies that there is the need for a communication channel that ends up to the View in addition to the one already in place, which originates from the View and is described by the MVVM model (see Figure 4-1). In this case, how do we solve this two-way communication requirement?

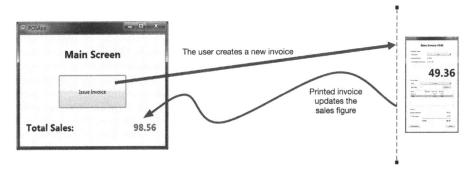

Figure 4-1. *Two-way communication requirement*

The Provider-Subscriber (ProSu) Framework

There are many acceptable approaches to address this new challenge. We could create a variable or even a property in the view of the InvoiceForm and directly link it to the label that represents the Total Sales figure in the MainScreenForm (LabelTotalSalesFigure). Then, before the InvoiceForm closes, it would update the LabelTotalSalesFigure with the new value. Although this is a common approach, we will opt out here, because that would create a tight linkage between two elements, leaving us with strong dependencies. Instead, we will turn to patterns that implement looser coupling among a different (and unknown) number of elements.

The pattern we will be looking at this section is usually referred to as the *observer* pattern. This is a one-to-many communication of change of states between objects that are loosely coupled. The pattern is well explored in a variety of sources, with the most notable being Gamma et. al. (1994). It's presented in Figure 4-2. In this pattern, a class that acts as provider of messages (or *publisher* as it is also called) sends messages to a number of classes (observers). The interpretation and, consequently, the course of action to be taken by the transmitted messages is the sole duty of the observer.

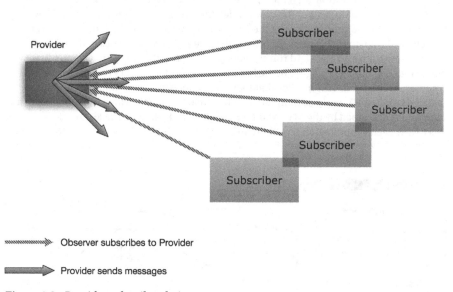

Observer subscribes to Provider

Provider sends messages

Figure 4-2. *Provider-subscriber design pattern*

For our needs, we are going to develop our own implementation instead of using a ready-made one. We shouldn't see this as restrictive; if we are familiar with an alternative implementation, feel free to use it.

Let's call this version the *ProSu Framework* (**Pro**vider-**Su**bscriber). For a number of reasons that don't fall in the scope of this book and this chapter, a very efficient and flexible way to implement this pattern is to employ interfaces.

■ **Note**   An interface works like a class that holds well-defined procedures and functions but doesn't provide the implementation of those methods; instead, it works as a blueprint to indicate what we should expect to see in terms of procedures and functions in a class that uses the interface. Interfaces are implemented in real classes and they allow the implementation of multi-inheritance classes in Delphi. If you need a refresher on the topic of interfaces, visit the documentation that comes with your version of Delphi or follow this resource (DocWiki, 2015).

Let's return to the `PosAppMVVMMainForm` project. The ProSu units will support our application. In order to keep our housekeeping at good levels, we will place them in separate folders.

1. Go to the folder where we have saved the project and the project group.

2. Create a new folder called `SupportCode`.

Figure 4-3 summarizes how the ProSu framework works. Any class (*subscriber*) that needs to follow messages from the provider subscribes to it using the `Subscribe` method of the provider (Step 1). Whenever the provider wants to alert the subscribers, it sends out a signal using the `NotifySubscriber` method (Step 2).

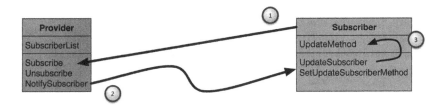

Figure 4-3. *Provider-subscriber implementation details*

This method invokes the `UpdateSubscriber` method at the subscriber side (Step 3). You will notice in Figure 4-3 that the subscriber has an `UpdateMethod` property and a `SetUpdateSubscriberMethod`. This is because we want to make the `subscriber` class to adapt to any classes in the code (as we want the same for the `provider` class). This means that the actual method the subscriber uses to respond to signals from the provider is not known in advance but it is class-dependent. `SetUpdateSubscriberMethod` and `UpdateMethod` provide a way to implement this, as we will see in the next lines of code. Overall, this adaptability of the framework to unknown classes is built on the flexibility of the interfaces. Now, let's dive into the code.

In the `POSAppMVVMMainForm` project, add a new unit called `Model.ProSu.Interfaces.pas`. (Remember? I said we'd try to keep the code as tidy as possible.) Save the unit in the `SourceCode` folder we created earlier. Then, add the following code.

```
unit Model.ProSu.Interfaces;

interface

uses
  Model.ProSu.InterfaceActions;

type
  INotificationClass = interface
    ['{2BB04DBB-6D61-4E4F-8C70-8BCC8E36FDE4}']
  end;

  TUpdateSubscriberMethod = procedure (const
notifyClass: INotificationClass) of object;

  ISubscriberInterface = interface
    ['{955BF992-F4FA-4141-9C0F-04600C582C00}']
    procedure UpdateSubscriber (const notifyClass: INotificationClass);
    procedure SetUpdateSubscriberMethod (newMethod:
TUpdateSubscriberMethod);
  end;

  IProviderInterface = interface
    ['{DD326AE1-5049-43AA-9215-DF53DB5FC958}']
    procedure Subscribe(const tmpSubscriber: ISubscriberInterface);
    procedure Unsubscribe(const tmpSubscriber: ISubscriberInterface);
    procedure NotifySubscribers (const notifyClass: INotificationClass);
  end;

implementation

end.
```

This is the GUID of the interface. In the IDE, press Ctrl+Shift+G to generate it

This is the footprint of the update method, which is invoked in the Subscriber

This unit defines the interfaces for the framework. Follow the same steps when we created the Model.ProSu.Interfaces.pas unit and create a new unit called Model.ProSu.Provider.pas with the following

```
unit Model.ProSu.Provider;

interface

uses Model.ProSu.Interfaces,
System.Generics.Collections;

type
 TProSuProvider = class (TInterfacedObject, IProviderInterface)
  private
    fSubscriberList: TList<ISubscriberInterface>;
  public
    procedure Subscribe(const tmpSubscriber:
ISubscriberInterface);
    procedure Unsubscribe(const tmpSubscriber: ISubscriberInterface);
    procedure NotifySubscribers (const notifyClass: INotificationClass);

    constructor Create;
    destructor Destroy; override;
  end;

implementation

{ TProSuProvider }

constructor TProSuProvider.Create;
begin
  inherited;
  fSubscriberList:=TList<ISubscriberInterface>.Create;
end;

destructor TProSuProvider.Destroy;
var
  iTemp: ISubscriberInterface;
begin
  for itemp in fSubscriberList do
      Unsubscribe(iTemp);
  fSubscriberList.Free;
  inherited;
end;

procedure TProSuProvider.NotifySubscribers(const notifyClass:
INotificationClass);
var
  tmpSubscriber: ISubscriberInterface;
```

We Include the interfaces we declared

This is how we attach an interface to a class

Holds references to the subscribers

63

```
begin
  for tmpSubscriber in fSubscriberList  do
    tmpSubscriber.UpdateSubscriber(notifyClass);
end;

procedure TProSuProvider.Subscribe(const tmpSubscriber:
ISubscriberInterface);
begin
  fSubscriberList.Add(tmpSubscriber);
end;

procedure TProSuProvider.Unsubscribe(const tmpSubscriber:
ISubscriberInterface);
begin
  fSubscriberList.Remove(tmpSubscriber);
end;

end.
```

We define the ProSuProvider class, which implements the IProviderInterface and represents the provider. We need a way to keep track of the subscribers and we'll do so by introducing a private TList variable. Then, we implement the Subscribe, Unsubscribe, and NotifySubscribers methods by manipulating the TList<T> property. Subscribe adds an interfaced subscriber to the list, Unsubscribe removes it, and NotifySubscribers invokes the UpdateSubscriber method of the subscriber. Apart from this, the Create and Destroy methods take care the fSubscriberList.

The last part of the framework deals with the subscriber. We need to create one more unit as we did earlier (Model.ProSu.Subscriber.pas) and implement it according to the following code. The subscriber unit is straightforward and simple.

```
unit Model.ProSu.Subscriber;

interface

uses Model.ProSu.Interfaces;

type
  TProSuSubscriber = class (TInterfacedObject, ISubscriberInterface)
  private
    fUpdateMethod: TUpdateSubscriberMethod;
  public
    procedure UpdateSubscriber (const notifyClass: INotificationClass);
    procedure SetUpdateSubscriberMethod (newMethod:
TUpdateSubscriberMethod);
  end;

implementation
```

```
{ TProSuSubscriber }

procedure TProSuSubscriber.SetUpdateSubscriberMethod(
  newMethod: TUpdateSubscriberMethod);
begin
  fUpdateMethod:=newMethod;
end;

procedure TProSuSubscriber.UpdateSubscriber(const notifyClass:
INotificationClass);
begin
  if Assigned(fUpdateMethod) then
    fUpdateMethod(notifyClass);
end;

end.
```

Two-Way Communication (Revisited)

We developed the *ProSu framework* as a response to the need we identified earlier for the View (MainForm) to receive notifications in addition to its ability to initiate communication with the ViewModel. The observer pattern does exactly this; it allows the View to receive notifications from the InvoiceForm to update the Total Sales figure.

Let's see how this works. We are going to use a simple form to imitate the functionality of printing an invoice and we will investigate how to make the MainForm update the sales figure. We can find the full code in the POSAppMVVMMainFormTest folder in the book's files.

1. Add a new form in the POSAppMVVMMainForm project, change the name to TestPrintInvoiceForm, and save it in the Views folder with the name View.TestPrintInvoice.pas.

2. Add a new button (TButton) rename it to ButtonPrintInvoice and change the text property to Print Invoice. The purpose of the button is to simulate the process of completing an invoice as we have it in the InvoiceForm. The TestPrintInvoice button will notify the MainForm with the new updated sales figure and will close the TestPrintInvoiceForm.

3. The design of the TestPrintInvoiceForm and the properties of the ButtonPrintInvoice are not important at this point.

4. Using Figures 4-1 and 4-3, we can draw comparisons and assign the role of the observer to the MainForm and the role of the provider to the TestPrintInvoiceForm in order to bring the two forms together under the ProSu paradigm.

Switch to the code view of the TestPrintInvoiceForm and declare a private variable as IProviderInterface, which is exposed as a read-only property. Then, add the following code to the FormCreate event. We also need to add the Model.ProSu. Interfaces and Model.ProSu.Provider units to the uses clauses.

```
interface

uses
  ..., Model.ProSu.Interfaces, Model.ProSu.Provider;

type
  TTestPrintInvoiceForm = class(TForm)
    ...
    procedure FormCreate(Sender: TObject);
  private
    fProvider: IProviderInterface;
  public
    property Provider: IProviderInterface read fProvider;
  end;

implementation

uses Model.ProSu.Provider;

procedure TTestPrintInvoiceForm.FormCreate(Sender: TObject);
begin
  fProvider:=TProSuProvider.Create;
end;
```

We don't need to release the fProvider in the FormDestroy event because interfaces manage their own lifecycles. What we need to do as the last step is write code in the OnClick event of the PrintInvoice button. The event will use the fProvider to update the subscribers. Basically, what we need to tell the subscribers has two parts: update the Total Sales figure's label and supply the new value of the total sales.

In order to achieve this, we need to look at the declaration of the NotifySubscribers in the Model.ProSu.Interfaces unit. The declaration of the method shows that we can only pass an INotificationClass interface parameter. This is quite fortunate as the implementation of the interface is totally abstract. Considering the flexibility of interfaces, what the INotifcationClass declaration tells us is that we can pass to the subscribers *any class we need* as long as it implements the INotificationClass interface, which by definition is empty.

Add a new unit to the project, save it in the SupportCode folder, and name it Model.ProSu.InterfaceActions. This unit will provide a reference to any actions we want subscribers to perform. Add the following code to this new unit.

```
unit Model.ProSu.InterfaceActions;

interface
```

```
type
  TInterfaceAction = (actUpdateTotalSalesFigure);
  TInterfaceActions = set of TInterfaceAction;

implementation

end.
```

The only thing we do in this unit is to declare available actions to the subscribers. At the moment, we have only one (UpdateTotalSalesFigure), but the following chapters will introduce more. We have also declared a set of actions in order to allow subscribers to perform more than one action with only one call from the provider.

We now need to declare the notification class. Open the Model.Declarations unit, add a reference to the Model.ProSu.InterfaceActions and Model.ProSu.Interfaces units, and declare the following class.

```
interface

uses
  ..., Model.ProSu.InterfaceActions, Model.ProSu.Interfaces;

type
  ...
  TNotificationClass = class (TInterfacedObject, INotificationClass)
  private
    faction: TInterfaceActions;          This tells the subscriber to
    factionValue: Double;                update the total sales label
  public
    property Actions: TInterfaceActions read fActions    This tells the
write fActions;                                          subscriber what
    property ActionValue: double read fActionValue write  the new updated
fActionValue;                                            value is
  end;
```

Back to the TestPrintInvoiceForm, implement the OnClick event of the ButtonPrintInvoice. We also need to add the Model.Declarations and Model.ProSu. InterfaceActions units.

```
interface

...

type
  TTestPrintInvoiceForm = class(TForm)
    ...
    procedure ButtonPrintInvoiceClick(Sender: TObject);
  private
```

```
  ...
  public
    ...
  end;

...
implementation
...

uses ..., Model.Declarations, Model.ProSu.InterfaceActions;

procedure TTestPrintInvoiceForm.ButtonPrintInvoiceClick(Sender: TObject);
var
  tmpNotificationClass: TNotificationClass;
begin
  tmpNotificationClass:=TNotificationClass.Create;
  try
    tmpNotificationClass.Actions:=[actUpdateTotalSalesFigure];
    tmpNotificationClass.ActionValue:=Random(1300);
    fProvider.NotifySubscribers(tmpNotificationClass);
  finally
    tmpNotificationClass.Free;
  end;
end;
```

It is time now to test whether the ProSu framework does the job. Open the View.MainForm unit and declare a new private variable to indicate that this form has the role of a subscriber in the ProSu domain.

```
interface

uses
  ..., Model.ProSu.Interfaces;

type
  TMainForm = class(TForm)
    ...
  private
    ...
    fSubscriber: ISubscriberInterface;
    ...
  public
    ...
  end;

...
implementation
...
```

```
uses
  Model.ProSu.Subscriber;

procedure TMainForm.FormCreate(Sender: TObject);
...
begin
  ...
  fSubscriber:=TProSuSubscriber.Create;
end;
```

Create the OnClick event of the ButtonInvoice and add the following code, which creates
the TestPrintInvoiceForm and subscribes the MainForm to it.

```
interface

uses
  ...

type
  TMainForm = class(TForm)
    ...
    procedure ButtonInvoiceClick(Sender: TObject);
  private
    ...
  public
    ...
  end;

...

implementation

...

uses View.TestPrintInvoice, Model.ProSu.Subscriber;

{ TMainForm }

procedure TMainForm.ButtonInvoiceClick(Sender: TObject);
var
  tmpTest: TTestPrintInvoiceForm;
begin
  tmpTest:=TTestPrintInvoiceForm.Create(self);
  tmpTest.Provider.Subscribe(fSubscriber);
  tmpTest.Show;
end;
```

*This allows the form
to receive
notifications from the
TestPrintInvoiceForm*

If we compile and execute POSAppMVVM, we will be able to open many test forms. However, we will not see the Total Sales figure label updated when we press the Print Invoice button. This is because, up to this point, we notify the subscriber (MainForm) regarding a change to the sales value, but we do not process this signal in the MainForm. In fact, we are one step behind the processing of the signal. The form is not yet aware that there is a message to be processed. This is what we are going to fix next.

When we developed the IProSuSubscriber interface and the TProSuSubscriber class, we implemented SetUpdateSubscriberMethod. This method will help us resolve the problem we are facing here. We need to declare a procedure in the subscriber (MainForm) and pass it to the provider; then, when a message needs to be delivered, the provider simply invokes this method.

In the View.MainForm unit, declare the NotificationFromProvider procedure and pass it to the provider.

```
interface

...

type
  TMainForm = class(TForm)
    ...
  private
    ...
    procedure NotificationFromProvider (const notifyClass:
INotificationClass);
  public
    ...
  end;

...

implementation

uses
    ..., Model.Declarations, Model.ProSu.InterfaceActions;


procedure TMainForm.FormCreate(Sender: TObject);
...
begin
  ...
  fSubscriber:=TProSuSubscriber.Create;
  fSubscriber.SetUpdateSubscriberMethod(NotificationFromProvider);
end;
```

This method uses the same declaration as the TUpdateSubscriberMethod in the Model.ProSu.Interfaces unit

Here we pass the method to the subscriber class

Now, we develop the NotificationFromProvider method to update the Total Sales figure label.

```
procedure TMainForm.NotificationFromProvider(
  const notifyClass: INotificationClass);
var
  tmpNotifClass: TNotificationClass;
begin
  if notifyClass is TNotificationClass then
  begin
    tmpNotifClass:=notifyClass as TNotificationClass;
    if actUpdateTotalSalesFigure in tmpNotifClass.Actions then
      LabelTotalSalesFigure.Text:=format('%10.2f',[tmpNotifClass.ActionValue]);

  end;
end;
```

We first translate notifyClass to TNotificationClass (typecast) and then check for the required action from the provider. If the action is actUpdateTotalSalesFigure, we update the Total Sales figure label. Compile and execute the application. Open a couple of invoice forms and click on the Print Invoice button. You should be able to see the Total Sales figure changing in the main form.

■ **Note**   The way we processed the message from the provider violates the MVVM design, as we bypassed the step where we retrieve the value from the ViewModel. Normally, we should call the UpdateTotalSalesFigure method. We didn't do this here because the aim was just to test the ProSu framework and confirm that messages can be passed back to the View. In the following material, we will revert to the use of the ViewModel.

We have tested the ProSu framework and now have the tools to establish two-way communication between the View and the ViewModel and, similarly, between the ViewModel and the Model. We don't need the TestPrintInvoiceForm unit any more, so you can either remove it from the project or just remove the code in the ButtonInvoiceClick method. In the code files that come with the book, you can load the POSAppMVVMInterfaces project.

Making the Code More Efficient

We have set up a way to organize the code, defined the different responsibilities and actions of the elements of the MVVM, and established two-way communication of the several elements. Before we move on and convert the InvoiceForm to the MVVM paradigm, I will discuss some changes to the code which allow for more efficient coding. This step is not vital for MVVM but it is good practice. It follows modern code architecture and fits nicely in our case. We will use interfaces extensively in the next chapter. This section introduces a form of structuring the code that hides the actual classes deep in the implementation section of the units and exposes them with interfaces.

■ **Note**   There are many articles and sources you can consult regarding the advantages of interfaces. I recommend reading this article (Hodges, 2016) and this excellent example of the S.O.L.I.D principles (Csaba, 2013). The latter article puts interfaces in a broader context in software development.

We'll start with the Model.Database unit and will expose the TDatabase class via an interface. In order to do this, we'll declare an interface in the interface section of the unit and will move the class declaration to the implementation section. Then, a function is required to access the class.

1.   Open Model.Database unit.

2.   Move the TDatabase declaration in the Implementation section.

3.   In the Interface section of the unit, declare this interface.

```
type
  IDatabaseInterface = interface
  ['{DDE3E13A-0EC5-4712-B068-9B510977CF71}']
    function GetCustomerList: TObjectList<TCustomer>;
    function GetCustomerFromName(const nameStr: string): TCustomer;
    function GetItems: TObjectList<TItem>;
    function GetItemFromDescription(const desc: string): TItem;
    function GetItemFromID(const id: Integer): TItem;
    function GetTotalSales: Currency;
    procedure SaveCurrentSales(const currentSales: Currency);
  end;
```

4.   Change the declaration part of TDatabase to the following:

```
type
  TDatabase = class (TInterfacedObject, IDatabaseInterface)
```

5.   In the Interface section, declare the following function:

```
function CreateDatabaseClass: IDatabaseInterface;
```

6.   In the Implementation section, develop the CreateDatabaseClass function:

```
function CreateDatabaseClass: IDatabaseInterface;
begin
  result:=TDatabase.Create;
end;
```

7. Every time we need a TDatabase class, we will declare the IDatabaseInterface and use the CreateDatabaseClass.

8. Open the Model.Main unit and change the type of fDatabase.

```
interface
...

type
  TMainModel = class
  private
    ...
    fDatabase: IDatabaseInterface;
  public
    ...
  end;
```

Replace TDatabase with IDatabaseInterface

9. In TMainModel.Create, change the line where your create the TDatabase class. Your code should look like this:

```
constructor TMainModel.Create;
begin

  fDatabase:=CreateDatabaseClass;
end;
```

Replace fDatabase:=TDatabase.Create with this

10. Interfaces don't need to be freed explicitly, as they can manage their lifecycle. This means that we don't need the fDatabase.Free line in the destructor of the TMainModel class. You can delete the whole destructor method.

Next, in the Model.Main unit, follow Steps to 2-9 in order to convert the TMainModel class. Your unit now looks like this:

```
unit Model.Main;

interface

uses Model.Declarations, Model.Database;

type
  IMainModelInterface = interface
  ['{345910DF-654D-43CF-BDE8-E708A9F33624}']
    function GetMainFormLabelsText: TMainFormLabelsText;
    function GetTotalSales: Currency;
  end;
```

73

```
function CreateMainModelClass: IMainModelInterface;

implementation

uses
  System.SysUtils;

type
  TMainModel = class (TInterfacedObject, IMainModelInterface)
  private
    fMainFormLabelsText: TMainFormLabelsText;
    fDatabase: IDatabaseInterface;
  public
    function GetMainFormLabelsText: TMainFormLabelsText;
    function GetTotalSales: Currency;
    constructor Create;
  end;

{ TMainModel }

...

function CreateMainModelClass: IMainModelInterface;
begin
  result:=TMainModel.Create;
end;
```

We now need to change the way we use IMainModel in the source code of the project (select the .exe file in the Project Manager and press Ctrl+V).

```
var
  mainModel: IMainModelInterface;      ◄──── Replace TMainModel with
                                              IMainModelInterface;

...
begin
  mainModel:=CreateMainModelClass;     ◄──── Replace
  mainViewModel:=TMainViewModel.Create;       mainModel:=TMainModel.Create
  mainViewModel.Model:=mainModel;             with this

  Application.Initialize;
    ...
end.
```

The last piece of code we need to change in order to accommodate the new way to use the TMainModel class is in ViewModel.Main.

```
unit ViewModel.Main;

interface

...

type
  TMainViewModel = class
  private
    fModel: IMainModelInterface;
    procedure SetModel (const newModel: IMainModelInterface);
    ...
  public
    property Model: IMainModelInterface read fModel write SetModel;
    ...
  end;

implementation

procedure TMainViewModel.SetModel(const newModel: IMainModelInterface);
begin
  fModel:=newModel;
end;
```

If you execute POSApp, you should be able to see the MainForm without getting any errors during the compilation. You can now change all the classes created so far using the approach we developed so far. I don't include all the changes here, as they are redundant and would take up lots of space. You can find the new versions of the files in the supplied code (POSAppMVVMMainFormFullInterfaces). In summary, these are the changes compared to the old code. The parentheses show the name of the interface and the name of the function that creates the class.

Model.ProSu.Provider:

1. Move TProSuProvider to the Implementation section.

2. Add a CreateProSuProviderClass function.

Model.ProSu.Subscriber:

1. Move TProSuSubscriber to the Implementation section.

2. Add a CreateProSuSubscriberClass function.

ViewModel.Main:

1. TMainViewModel (IMainViewModelInterface; CreateMainViewModelClass)

2. Property Model has a getter GetModel function.

3. Property LabelsText has a getter GetLabelsText function.

75

View.MainForm:

1. The fViewModel property in the TMainForm class is declared as IMainViewModelInterface.

2. The fSubscriber property in the TMainForm class is declared as ISubscriberInterface.

3. The property ViewModel is declared as IMainViewModelInterface.

4. Use procedure SetViewModel (const newViewModel: IMainViewModelInterface) in both the definition of the class and the implementation of the procedure.

5. In the project file, change the declaration of mainViewModel:

```
var
    ...
mainViewModel: IMainViewModelInterface;
```

6. In the project file, mainViewModel:=CreateMainViewModelClass;

7. In TMainForm.Create, fSubscriber:= CreateProSuSubscriberClass;

8. Remove the TMainForm.FormDestroy event.

One last move before we continue to the InvoiceForm; when we developed the ProSu units, we created a dedicated unit to keep all the declarations of the interfaces. This is good practice and now we will also move the interface declarations of the Model, the ViewModel, and the database to a new unit.

1. Create a new unit and save it as Model.Interfaces in the Models folder.

2. Move the IDatabaseInterface declaration from the Model. Database unit to the Model.Interfaces unit.

3. Add the Model.Declarations unit in the uses clause of Model.Databases.

4. Add System.Generics.Collections in the uses clause of Model.Interfaces.

5. Add Model.Interfaces in the Implementation uses clause of Model.Main.

6. Move the IMainModelInterface declaration from the Model. Main unit to Model.Interfaces unit.

7. Add the `Model.Interfaces` unit in the `Interface` uses clause of `Model.Main`.

8. Add the `Model.Interfaces` unit in the `Implementation` uses clause of `ViewModel.Main`.

9. Move the `IMainViewModelInterface` declaration from the `ViewModel.Main` unit to the `Model.Interfaces` unit.

10. Add the `Model.Interfaces` unit in the uses clause of the `View.MainForm` file.

■ **Note** At this stage, we have organized our code into small, manageable units. Interfaces helped a lot in this regard. We converted all the core classes that are linked to the MVVM; however, we didn't touch the classes in the `Model.Declarations` unit. In a real-world application, you may also want to use interfaces for those classes. In the rest of the book, we will use the original version of `Model.Declarations` (without interfaces), because converting those classes to use interfaces requires additional work that is not related to the scope of this book. This can be a challenge to you!

Summary

The ProSu framework (observer pattern) provides a way to establish bi-directional communication between the different components of the MVVM. Basic implementation of S.O.L.I.D principles and the knowledge and methodology we developed in the previous chapters provide the tools to continue the conversion of the last part of the application, the `InvoiceForm`. This is the focus of the next chapter.

References

Csaba, P., 2013. "The SOLID Principles: Envato Tuts+ Code Tutorials," available at http://code.tutsplus.com/series/the-solid-principles--cms-634.

DocWiki, 2015. "Interface References (Delphi)," available at http://docwiki. embarcadero.com/RADStudio/Seattle/en/Interface_References [Accessed 08/07/ 2016].

Gamma, E., Helm, R., Johnson, R., Vlissidis, J., and Booch, G., 1994. *Design Patterns: Elements of Resusable Object-Oriented Software,* Addison-Wesley Professional.

Hodges, N., 2016. "Why you Should Be Using Interfaces and Not Direct References," Available at http://www.nickhodges.com/page/Why-You-Should-be-Using-Interfaces-and-not-Direct-References.aspx [Accessed 24/06/2016].

CHAPTER 5

■ ■ ■

Converting the InvoiceForm

In the previous chapters, we developed a methodology to guide us in converting an application to follow the MVVM design. In summary, those steps are the following:

1. Identify the different tasks for each procedure, class, and view the application performs.

2. Identify which of those tasks are duties of the Model, the ViewModel, and the View, according to the MVVM paradigm.

3. Consider moving procedures and functions from the View to the ViewModel and the Model.

4. Build the required links to make the new code functional on the normal direction View-ViewModel-Model by developing the necessary properties, procedures, and functions.

5. Add functionality to the new code to support two-way communication between the View-ViewModel-Model according to the design needs of the application.

The View of the InvoiceForm

This section starts the convertion of the InvoiceForm by parameterizing the labels and the button captions of the form, as we did with the main screen. Figure 5-1 shows how the View retrieves the captions of the labels and buttons from the ViewModel and the Model. The approach is similar to Figure 3-1. We will also use dummy label values as we did before (Figure 3-1).

Follow these steps:

1. Open the project you developed in the previous chapter or load POSAppMVVMFullInterfaces from the code files that come with the book.

© John Kouraklis 2016
J. Kouraklis, *MVVM in Delphi*, DOI 10.1007/978-1-4842-2214-0_5

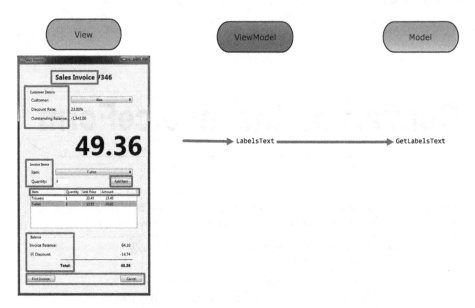

Figure 5-1. InvoiceForm in the MVVM design

2. Add a new form to the project and save it as `View.InvoiceForm` in the Views folder.

3. Open the form in the IDE and add the components (labels, group boxes, and buttons) as you did in Figure 2-6 using "dummy" labels.

■ **Tip** In the book's code files, you will find the `InvoiceForm` files (`View.InvoiceForm.fmx` and `View.InvoiceForm.pas`) in the `Thin Forms` folder. For convenience, you can import them into your project instead of creating the form from scratch.

---

4. Open `View.MainForm`, click on the `ButtonInvoice` button, and add the following code to the `ButtonInvoiceClick` event. You also need to add the `View.InvoiceForm` in the Implementation uses clause.

```
unit View.MainForm;

interface

...

type
```

```
TMainForm = class(TForm)
  ...
  procedure ButtonInvoiceClick(Sender: TObject);
  ...
end;

...

implementation

uses
  ..., View.InvoiceForm;

{$R *.fmx}

{ TMainForm }

procedure TMainForm.ButtonInvoiceClick(Sender: TObject);
var
  tmpInvoiceForm: TSalesInvoiceForm;
begin
  tmpInvoiceForm:=TSalesInvoiceForm.Create(self);
  try
    tmpInvoiceForm.ShowModal;
  finally
    tmpInvoiceForm.Free;
  end;
end;

...

end.
```

If you compile and run the project at this stage, you can click on the Issue Invoice button in the main screen and get the invoice form with the "dummy" labels.

■ **Tip**   In the code files, you can open the POSAppMVVMStart project. This project implements the previous steps and you can use it to work on the changes introduced in the following pages. The POSAppMVVMInvoiceForm project includes the changes we will incorporate in this chapter.

The Model of the InvoiceForm

We now need to provide the captions and the text for InvoiceForm's labels. As explained, we will use the same approach we implemented when we considered how to allow translations of the label captions in the MainScreen form.

Open the Model.Declarations unit and define a record to keep the labels' values and the buttons' captions. You can use Figure 5-1 as a guide.

```
unit Model.Declarations;

interface

...

type
  ...

  TInvoiceFormLabelsText = record
    Title,
    CustomerDetailsGroupText,
    CustomerText,
    CustomerDiscountRateText,
    CustomerOutstandingBalanceText,

    InvoiceItemsGroupText,
    InvoiceItemsText,
    InvoiceItemsQuantityText,
    InvoiceItemsAddItemButtonText,
    InvoiceItemsGridItemText,
    InvoiceItemsGridQuantityText,
    InvoiceItemsGridUnitPriceText,
    InvoiceItemsGridAmountText,

    BalanceGroupText,
    BalanceInvoiceBalanceText,
    BalanceDiscountText,
    BalanceTotalText,

    PrintInvoiceButtonText,
    PrintingText,
    CancelButtonText: string;
  end;

implementation
...

end.
```

1. Create a new unit and save it as Model.Invoice.pas under the Models folder. This hosts the Model of the InvoiceForm.

2. Load the Model.Interfaces unit and declare a new interface for the Model of the invoice form. For now, we need only one function, which provides access to the labels of the form.

```
unit Model.Interfaces;

interface

...

type
  ...

  IInvoiceModelInterface = interface
    ['{A286914B-7979-4726-8D9C-18865B47CD12}']
    function GetInvoiceFormLabelsText: TInvoiceFormLabelsText;
  end;

implementation

end.
```

3. In the Model.Invoice unit, add the following code. We define the class for the Model of the invoice form and a function to allow access.

```
unit Model.Invoice;

interface

uses
  Model.Interfaces;

function CreateInvoiceModelClass: IInvoiceModelInterface;

implementation

uses
  Model.Declarations;

type
  TInvoiceModel = class (TInterfacedObject, IInvoiceModelInterface)
  private
    fInvoiceFormLabelsText: TInvoiceFormLabelsText;
```

```
  public
    function GetInvoiceFormLabelsText: TInvoiceFormLabelsText;
  end;

function CreateInvoiceModelClass: IInvoiceModelInterface;
begin
  result:=TInvoiceModel.Create;
end;

{ TInvoiceModel }

function TInvoiceModel.GetInvoiceFormLabelsText: TInvoiceFormLabelsText;
begin
  fInvoiceFormLabelsText.Title:='Sales Invoice';
  fInvoiceFormLabelsText.CustomerDetailsGroupText:='Customer Details';
  fInvoiceFormLabelsText.CustomerText:='Customer:';
  fInvoiceFormLabelsText.CustomerDiscountRateText:='Discount Rate:';
  fInvoiceFormLabelsText.CustomerOutstandingBalanceText:='Outstanding
Balance:';

  fInvoiceFormLabelsText.InvoiceItemsGroupText:='Invoice Items';
  fInvoiceFormLabelsText.InvoiceItemsText:='Item:';
  fInvoiceFormLabelsText.InvoiceItemsQuantityText:='Quantity:';
  fInvoiceFormLabelsText.InvoiceItemsAddItemButtonText:='Add Item';

  fInvoiceFormLabelsText.InvoiceItemsGridItemText:='Item';
  fInvoiceFormLabelsText.InvoiceItemsGridQuantityText:='Quantity';
  fInvoiceFormLabelsText.InvoiceItemsGridUnitPriceText:='Unit Price';
  fInvoiceFormLabelsText.InvoiceItemsGridAmountText:='Amount';

  fInvoiceFormLabelsText.BalanceGroupText:='Balance';
  fInvoiceFormLabelsText.BalanceInvoiceBalanceText:='Invoice Balance:';
  fInvoiceFormLabelsText.BalanceDiscountText:='Discount';
  fInvoiceFormLabelsText.BalanceTotalText:='Total:';

  fInvoiceFormLabelsText.PrintInvoiceButtonText:='Print Invoice';
  fInvoiceFormLabelsText.PrintingText:='Printing Invoice…';
  fInvoiceFormLabelsText.CancelButtonText:='Cancel';

  result:=fInvoiceFormLabelsText;
end;

end.
```

The ViewModel of the InvoiceForm

We have created the two side components of the design (Model and View). Now we need to bring these two together. This is the job of the ViewModel of the invoice form, which will fetch the labels and the captions from the Model and feed them to the View. In order for this to happen, we need access to the Model and a way to retrieve the labels. We will do the last part by declaring a property.

1. Open the Model.Interfaces unit and declare the appropriate interface.

```
unit Model.Interfaces;

interface
...

type
  IInvoiceViewModelInterface = interface
    ['{87D2F27E-8B33-46C5-B44C-DBFC58A871BC}']
    function GetModel: IInvoiceModelInterface;
    procedure SetModel(const newModel: IInvoiceModelInterface);
    function GetLabelsText: TInvoiceFormLabelsText;
    property Model: IInvoiceModelInterface read GetModel write SetModel;
    property LabelsText: TInvoiceFormLabelsText read GetLabelsText;
  end;

implementation

end.
```

2. Create a new unit called ViewModel.Invoice and develop the ViewModel as per the following code.

```
unit ViewModel.Invoice;

interface

uses
  Model.Interfaces;

function CreateInvoiceViewModelClass: IInvoiceViewModelInterface;

implementation

uses
  Model.Declarations;
```

```
type
  TInvoiceViewModel = class(TInterfacedObject, IInvoiceViewModelInterface)
  private
    fModel: IInvoiceModelInterface;
    fLabelsText: TInvoiceFormLabelsText;
    function GetModel: IInvoiceModelInterface;
    procedure SetModel(const newModel: IInvoiceModelInterface);
    function GetLabelsText: TInvoiceFormLabelsText;
  public
    property Model: IInvoiceModelInterface read GetModel write SetModel;
    property LabelsText: TInvoiceFormLabelsText read GetLabelsText;
  end;

function CreateInvoiceViewModelClass: IInvoiceViewModelInterface;
begin
  result:=TInvoiceViewModel.Create;
end;

{ TInvoiceViewModel }

function TInvoiceViewModel.GetLabelsText: TInvoiceFormLabelsText;
begin
    result:=fModel.GetInvoiceFormLabelsText;
end;

function TInvoiceViewModel.GetModel: IInvoiceModelInterface;
begin
  result:=fModel;
end;

procedure TInvoiceViewModel.SetModel(const newModel:
IInvoiceModelInterface);
begin
  fModel:=newModel;
end;

end.
```

This code follows the design patterns we developed in the previous chapters—it uses interfaces, hides the class implementation inside the units, and creates loose connections between the View, the ViewModel, and the Model.

Retrieving the Labels from the ViewModel

We are now ready to update the invoice form with the labels and the captions as they are provided by the ViewModel. Switch to the View.InvoiceForm unit and add the following code.

```
unit View.InvoiceForm;

interface

uses
  ..., Model.Interfaces;

type
  TSalesInvoiceForm = class(TForm)
    ...
  private
    fViewModel: IInvoiceViewModelInterface;
    procedure SetViewModel (const newViewModel: IInvoiceViewModelInterface);
    procedure UpdateLabels;
  public
    property ViewModel: IInvoiceViewModelInterface read fViewModel write
SetViewModel;
  end;

implementation

{$R *.fmx}

{ TSalesInvoiceForm }

procedure TSalesInvoiceForm.SetViewModel(
  const newViewModel: IInvoiceViewModelInterface);
begin
  fViewModel:=newViewModel;
  if not Assigned(fViewModel) then
    raise Exception.Create('Sales Invoice View Model is required');
UpdateLabels;
end;

procedure TSalesInvoiceForm.UpdateLabels;
begin
  LabelTitle.Text:=fViewModel.LabelsText.Title;

GroupBoxCustomerDetails.Text:=fViewModel.LabelsText.CustomerDetailsGroupText;
```

Reference to the ViewModel

```
LabelCustomer.Text:=fViewModel.LabelsText.CustomerText;
LabelDiscountRate.Text:=fViewModel.LabelsText.CustomerDiscountRateText;
LabelOutstandingBalance.Text:=fViewModel.LabelsText.CustomerOutstandingBalan
ceText;
GroupBoxInvoiceItems.Text:=fViewModel.LabelsText.InvoiceItemsGroupText;
LabelItem.Text:=fViewModel.LabelsText.InvoiceItemsText;
LabelQuantity.Text:=fViewModel.LabelsText.InvoiceItemsQuantityText;
ButtonAddItem.Text:=fViewModel.LabelsText.InvoiceItemsAddItemButtonText;
StringColumn1.Header:=fViewModel.LabelsText.InvoiceItemsGridItemText;
StringColumn2.Header:=fViewModel.LabelsText.InvoiceItemsGridQuantityText;
StringColumn3.Header:=fViewModel.LabelsText.InvoiceItemsGridUnitPriceText;
StringColumn4.Header:=fViewModel.LabelsText.InvoiceItemsGridAmountText;

GroupBoxBalance.Text:=fViewModel.LabelsText.BalanceGroupText;
LabelInvBalance.Text:=fViewModel.LabelsText.BalanceInvoiceBalanceText;
CheckBoxDiscount.Text:=fViewModel.LabelsText.BalanceDiscountText;
LabelTotal.Text:=fViewModel.LabelsText.BalanceTotalText;

ButtonPrintInvoice.Text:=fViewModel.LabelsText.PrintInvoiceButtonText;
LabelPrinting.Text:=fViewModel.LabelsText.PrintingText;
ButtonCancel.Text:=fViewModel.LabelsText.CancelButtonText;

end;

end.
```

This code will change the labels and the captions of the components of the form but only when we make the form, the ViewModel, and the Model aware of each other. In the View. MainForm unit, update the ButtonInvoiceClick event to create the different elements.

```
...
implementation

uses
...,
Model.Invoice, ViewModel.Invoice;

...

procedure TMainForm.ButtonInvoiceClick(Sender: TObject);
var
  ...                                              The Model of the form
  invoiceModel: IInvoiceModelInterface;   ◄─────────
  invoiceViewModel: IInvoiceViewModelInterface;  ◄───────The ViewModel
begin                                                      of the form
  invoiceModel:=CreateInvoiceModelClass;  ◄─────────
  invoiceViewModel:=CreateInvoiceViewModelClass; ◄──────Here we create the
  invoiceViewModel.Model:=invoiceModel; ◄──────         Model and the
                                                         ViewModel

  tmpInvoiceForm:=TSalesInvoiceForm.Create(self);
  tmpInvoiceForm.ViewModel:=invoiceViewModel; ◄────────Here we assign the
  try                                                   Model to the
    ...                                                 ViewModel
  end;
end;
```

If you execute POSApp, you should be able to see the correct labels and captions in the invoice form. There are a few points in the code to note:

- The ButtonInvoiceClick event declares the Model, the ViewModel, and the View of the invoice form as local variables. There are many developers who think that the Model and the ViewModel should be declared as private variables of the form. There is no doubt this can also be done. My choice is to use local variables because I prefer to have organized and neat code whenever the scope of the variables is limited, as it is in this case.

- In the same event, we independently create the Model, the ViewModel, and the View and then continue with the assignments. This is one approach to the issue of the order of creation. In the MVVM community, there are discussions regarding which part of the pattern you create next (View-ViewModel-Model). For example, in this case, you could create the ViewModel and assign it to the form. The ViewModel would then create the Model and assign it to itself. This approach has its place in MVVM coding, but it is not always easy to implement.

- The task of retrieving the values of the labels and the captions from the Model is quite trivial. As you can observe, in this case, the ViewModel just passes the values from the Model to the View without any processing. In the broader community of developers (not only among Delphi programmers), many feel that in cases like this, the MVVM pattern generates additional coding without offering any significant advantages. Sometimes, they refer to such situations with the term *boilerplate code*. It may be true that there are simple cases in which MVVM does not appear to increase efficiency. In general, MVVM thrives whenever significant manipulation of data and information is required to generate loosely coupled, complex outputs and sophisticated user interfaces. The pattern performs well in such cases because it offers a middle layer (ViewModel) that gives space to developers to maneuver according to their needs without touching the Model or the View. For example, in the case with the labels, imagine you have two separate models that offer English and Greek labels but that the Greek translation is incomplete. The ViewModel could retrieve the Greek labels and fill in the gaps from the English model.

Setting Up the Invoice Form

Following the current methodology, before we break up the different parts of the form to meet the MVVM design rules, we need to identify which steps the form is implementing. Looking at the FormCreate event, you can see that there are two major components that are being initialized when the form is created—the classes and the graphical elements of the form (see Figure 5-2).

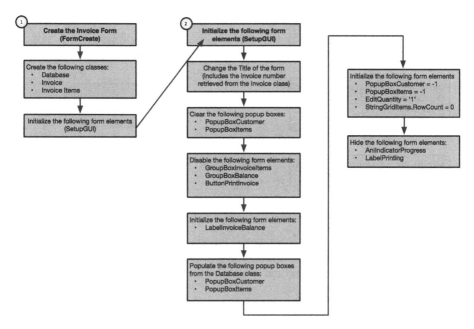

Figure 5-2. *Initial set up of InvoiceForm*

FormCreate initializes the required classes to track an invoice (the database, invoice, and invoice items classes). Then, the SetupGUI procedure is called, which changes the title of the form, initializes the popup boxes (the customer and items), disables the invoice items (the group box, the balance group box, and the Print Invoice button), and initializes the invoice balance label. The procedure then retrieves the customer and items lists from the database, populates the lists in the relevant popup boxes, and sets the initial values of those elements. It sets the quantity to one, clears the grid and, then hides the animated indicator and the label with the "Printing..." text.

Next, we need to clarify which components of the MVVM pattern are responsible for performing these tasks. This may be straightforward in some cases, but in other situations a more complicated approach may be required. Figure 5-3 inspects the FormCreate event and identifies that the event defines three classes that are part of the business logic (the Model) of the invoice form. Therefore, we need to declare and initialize these classes in the Model.

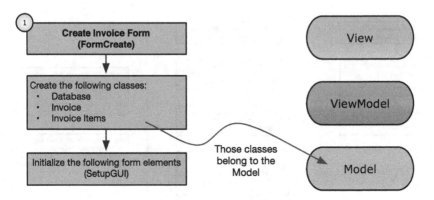

Figure 5-3. *The FormCreate event in the MVVM design*

Open the Model.Invoice unit and declare the following variables in the private section of the TInvoiceModel class. You also need to add System.Generics.Collections in the Implementation uses clause and implement the constructor and the destructor of the class.

```
unit Model.Invoice;

interface

...

implementation

uses
  ..., System.Generics.Collections;

type
  TInvoiceModel = class (TInterfacedObject, IInvoiceModelInterface)
  private
    ...
    fDatabase: IDatabaseInterface;
    fInvoice: TInvoice;
    fCurrentInvoiceItems: TObjectList<TInvoiceItem>;
  public
    ...
    constructor Create;
    destructor Destroy; override;
  end;
```

```
constructor TInvoiceModel.Create;
begin
  fDatabase:=CreateDatabaseClass;
  fInvoice:=TInvoice.Create;
  fInvoice.ID:=1;
  fInvoice.Number:=Random(3000);
  fCurrentInvoiceItems:=TObjectList<TInvoiceItem>.Create;
end;

destructor TInvoiceModel.Destroy;
begin
  fCurrentInvoiceItems.Free;
  fInvoice.Free;
  inherited;
end;
```

■ **Note**   In the Create event, we used an interfaced class for the TDatabase but a normal class for the TInvoice. This is because we decided in Chapter 4 to keep that class (and a few others) in their normal form.

You may also notice that we use a new database class in the TInvoiceModel class. This means that every time an invoice form is created, a new database class is going to be instantiated as well. Admittedly, this is not optimal design for a line-of-business application. In such cases, you typically have a separate class that provides access to the database and you *inject* it into every class, component, or procedure that requires access to the database. In some cases, you may keep the database connection open during the lifetime of the application. In POSApp, the database class is very generic and limited in scope, but it allows us to focus on the design pattern.

FormCreate calls SetupGUI procedure, which changes the title label of the invoice form to include the invoice number (see Figure 5-4). Changing the title is something that falls under the View and the invoice number comes from the Model. The choice of including the invoice number in the title is a very simple example of what is called *View state* and it is performed by the ViewModel.

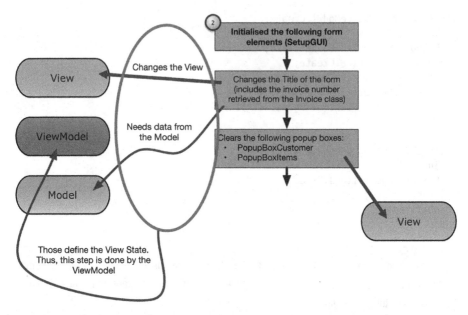

Figure 5-4. *The first part of SetupGUI in MVVM*

Open the Model.Interfaces unit and add the following function and property to the declarations of IInvoiceModelInterface and IInvoiceViewModelInterface.

```
type
  ...
  IInvoiceModelInterface = interface
    ...
    procedure SetInvoice(const newInvoice: TInvoice);
    procedure GetInvoice(var invoice: TInvoice);
  end;
  ...
  IInvoiceViewModelInterface = interface
    ...
    function GetTitleText: string;
    ...
    property TitleText: string read GetTitleText;
  end;
```

Move to the Model.Invoice unit and develop the GetInvoice and SetInvoice procedures as in the following code. Then, open ViewModel.Invoice and create the GetTitleText.

```
unit Model.Invoice;

interface
```

```
...

implementation

...

type
  TInvoiceModel = class (TInterfacedObject, IInvoiceModelInterface)
    ...
    public
      ...
      procedure SetInvoice(const newInvoice: TInvoice);
      procedure GetInvoice(var invoice: TInvoice);
    end;

...

procedure TInvoiceModel.GetInvoice(var invoice: TInvoice);
begin
  invoice:=fInvoice;
end;

procedure TInvoiceModel.SetInvoice(const newInvoice: TInvoice);
begin
  fInvoice:=newInvoice;
end;

...

end.

unit ViewModel.Invoice;

interface

...

implementation

...

type
  TInvoiceViewModel = class(TInterfacedObject, IInvoiceViewModelInterface)
    private
      ...
      function GetTitleText: string;
    public
      ...
```

```
  end;

...

function TInvoiceViewModel.GetTitleText: string;
var
  tmpInvoice: TInvoice;
begin
  fModel.GetInvoice(tmpInvoice);
  result:=fModel.GetInvoiceFormLabelsText.Title+' #'+IntToStr(tmpInvoice.
Number)

end;

...

end.
```

GetTitleText creates the correct title for the InvoiceForm by accessing the invoice
Model. The last step we need to implement is to call GetTitleText from the InvoiceForm.
In the View.InvoiceForm, create a new private procedure called SetupGUI. In the initial
version of the invoice form, SetupGUI is called in the constructor of the form. In this
implementation, this will not work because we assign the ViewModel of the invoice
form after we create the form. The appropriate location to call SetupGUI is at the end of
the assignment of the ViewModel (SetViewModel). In addition, according to Figure 5-4,
SetupGUI clears the two popup boxes and the string grid and sets the default value of the
quantity edit field.

```
 unit View.InvoiceForm;

interface

...

type
  TSalesInvoiceForm = class(TForm)
    ...
  private
    ...
    procedure SetupGUI;
  public
    ...
  end;

implementation

...

procedure TSalesInvoiceForm.SetupGUI;
begin
  LabelTitle.Text:=fViewModel.TitleText;
  PopupBoxCustomer.Clear;
  PopupBoxItems.Clear;
  StringGridItems.RowCount:=0;
  EditQuantity.Text:='1';
end;

procedure TSalesInvoiceForm.SetViewModel(
  const newViewModel: IInvoiceViewModelInterface);
begin
  ...
  SetupGUI;
end;
```

Here we retrieve the title from the ViewModel

Run POSApp and open an invoice form. You can now see the number of the invoice at the top of the form.

Disabling and Hiding Elements

The rest of the actions in the original SetupGUI follow the pattern used to update the title of the InvoiceForm. This section looks at how we can disable and hide elements of the form. Disabling and hiding are two states of the View components. Therefore, they represent view state and, as a consequence, they must be controlled by the ViewModel. It is this ViewModel which determines the View state by looking at data from the Model.

Open Model.Interfaces and declare the following properties and functions in IInvoiceViewModelInterface.

```
...

IInvoiceViewModelInterface = interface
    ...
    function GetGroupBoxInvoiceItemsEnabled: Boolean;
    function GetGroupBoxBalanceEnabled: Boolean;
    function GetButtonPrintInvoiceEnabled: Boolean;
    function GetAniIndicatorProgressVisible: Boolean;
    function GetLabelPrintingVisible: Boolean;

    ...

    property GroupBoxInvoiceItemsEnabled: boolean read
GetGroupBoxInvoiceItemsEnabled;
    property GroupBoxBalanceEnabled: boolean read GetGroupBoxBalanceEnabled;
    property ButtonPrintInvoiceEnabled: Boolean read
GetButtonPrintInvoiceEnabled;
    property AniIndicatorProgressVisible: Boolean read
GetAniIndicatorProgressVisible;
    property LabelPrintingVisible: Boolean read GetLabelPrintingVisible;
  end;
```

Then, write the implementations of these functions in the ViewModel.Invoice unit. In this unit, you need to create the constructor of the class in order to set up the initial state of the components.

```
unit ViewModel.Invoice;

interface

...

implementation

...

type
  TInvoiceViewModel = class(TInterfacedObject, IInvoiceViewModelInterface)
  private
```

```
    ...
    fInvoiceItemsEnabled,
    fBalanceEnabled,
    fPrintButtonEnabled,
    fAniIndicatorVisible,
    fPrintingLabelVisible: boolean;
    ...
    function GetGroupBoxInvoiceItemsEnabled: Boolean;
    function GetGroupBoxBalanceEnabled: Boolean;
    function GetButtonPrintInvoiceEnabled: Boolean;
    function GetAniIndicatorProgressVisible: Boolean;
    function GetLabelPrintingVisible: Boolean;
  public
    constructor Create;
    ...
  end;

...

{ TInvoiceViewModel }

constructor TInvoiceViewModel.Create;
begin
  fInvoiceItemsEnabled:=false;
  fBalanceEnabled:=false;
  fPrintButtonEnabled:=false;
  fAniIndicatorVisible:=false;
  fPrintingLabelVisible:=false;
end;

function TInvoiceViewModel.GetAniIndicatorProgressVisible: Boolean;
begin
  result:=fAniIndicatorVisible;
end;

function TInvoiceViewModel.GetButtonPrintInvoiceEnabled: Boolean;
begin
  result:=fPrintButtonEnabled;
end;

function TInvoiceViewModel.GetGroupBoxBalanceEnabled: Boolean;
begin
  result:=fBalanceEnabled;
end;

function TInvoiceViewModel.GetGroupBoxInvoiceItemsEnabled: Boolean;
begin
  Result:=fInvoiceItemsEnabled;
end;
```

99

```
function TInvoiceViewModel.GetLabelPrintingVisible: Boolean;
begin
  result:=fPrintingLabelVisible;
end;
...

end.
```

View.InvoiceForm includes two procedures—UpdateGroups and UpdatePrinting. This gives us the flexibility to update the printing labels independently of the groups. The initial call of the procedures is done in SetViewModel.

```
unit View.InvoiceForm;

interface

...

type
  TSalesInvoiceForm = class(TForm)
    ...
  private
    ...
    procedure UpdateGroups;
    procedure UpdatePrintingStatus;
  public
    ...
  end;

implementation

...

procedure TSalesInvoiceForm.SetViewModel(
  const newViewModel: IInvoiceViewModelInterface);
begin
  ...
  UpdateGroups;
  UpdatePrintingStatus;
end;

procedure TSalesInvoiceForm.UpdateGroups;
begin
  GroupBoxInvoiceItems.Enabled:=fViewModel.GroupBoxInvoiceItemsEnabled;
  GroupBoxBalance.Enabled:=fViewModel.GroupBoxBalanceEnabled;
  ButtonPrintInvoice.Enabled:=fViewModel.ButtonPrintInvoiceEnabled;
end;
```

```
procedure TSalesInvoiceForm.UpdatePrintingStatus;
begin
  AniIndicatorProgress.Visible:=fViewModel.AniIndicatorProgressVisible;
  LabelPrinting.Visible:=fViewModel.LabelPrintingVisible;
end;

...

end.
```

Getting the Customer and Items Lists

We follow similar steps as before in order to get the lists of the customers and the items. We start from the interface of the Model.Invoice unit, where we expose procedures to retrieve data from the database. Then, we declare new properties and procedures in the ViewModel.Invoice interface and develop the relevant code in the units.

```
unit Model.Interfaces
...

IInvoiceModelInterface = interface
    ['{A286914B-7979-4726-8D9C-18865B47CD12}']
    function GetInvoiceFormLabelsText: TInvoiceFormLabelsText;
    procedure SetInvoice(const newInvoice: TInvoice);
    procedure GetInvoice(var invoice: TInvoice);
    procedure GetCustomerList(var customers: TObjectList<TCustomer>);
    procedure GetItems(var items: TObjectList<TItem>);
  end;

  IInvoiceViewModelInterface = interface
    procedure GetCustomerList(var customers: TObjectList<TCustomer>);
    procedure GetItems(var items: TObjectList<TItem>);
    ...
  end;
...
end.

unit Model.Invoice;

interface

...

implementation

...
```

```
type
  TInvoiceModel = class (TInterfacedObject, IInvoiceModelInterface)
  private
    ...
  public
    ...
    procedure GetCustomerList(var customers: TObjectList<TCustomer>);
    procedure GetItems(var items: TObjectList<TItem>);
  end;

...

procedure TInvoiceModel.GetCustomerList(var customers:
TObjectList<TCustomer>);
begin
  customers:=fDatabase.GetCustomerList
end;

procedure TInvoiceModel.GetItems(var items: TObjectList<TItem>);
begin
  items:=fDatabase.GetItems
end;

...

end.

unit ViewModel.Invoice;

interface

...

implementation

...

type
  TInvoiceViewModel = class(TInterfacedObject, IInvoiceViewModelInterface)
  private
    ...
    procedure GetCustomerList(var customers: TObjectList<TCustomer>);
    procedure GetItems(var items: TObjectList<TItem>);
  public
    ...
  end;

...
```

```
procedure TInvoiceViewModel.GetCustomerList(
  var customers: TObjectList<TCustomer>);
begin
  if not Assigned(fModel) then
    Exit;
  fModel.GetCustomerList(customers);
end;

procedure TInvoiceViewModel.GetItems(var items: TObjectList<TItem>);
begin
  if not Assigned(fModel) then
    Exit;
  fModel.GetItems(items);
end;

end.
```

Summary

In this chapter, we started bringing the tools and skills developed in the previous chapters together. We formalized a methodology to convert code to the MVVM pattern and started applying it to the InvoiceForm. This transformation looked at content that does not change according to user interactions. In the following chapter, we will learn how to make the MVVM responsive to user events.

CHAPTER 6

User Interaction

Views (including forms, the console, and other means of data presentation) are created to present information and data to users and to allow them to interact with the software. User interaction is an integral part of every design pattern, including MVVM. As presented in Chapter 4, the way this project implements two-way communication between the different elements of the pattern is by using the Provider-Subscriber (ProSu) framework. In this chapter, we learn how to put ProSu into action and implement user interaction.

Selecting a Customer

When the user selects a customer from the popup box, POSApp retrieves the discount rate and the outstanding balance from the database and updates the relevant fields in the InvoiceForm. It enables the group boxes for the invoice items and the balances, clears the grid of any items left, and resets the discount check box.

1. Following Figure 4-2, the *View* (InvoiceForm) works as the subscriber and the *ViewModel* is the provider. Use the project we developed in the previous chapter or open POSAppMVVMInvoiceForm from the code that comes with the book. Go to Model.Interfaces and declare a property to hold the provider class and a getter method. We also need to add the relevant units in the uses section.

```
unit Model.Interfaces;

interface

uses
  ..., Model.ProSu.Interfaces;

type
  ...
  IInvoiceViewModelInterface = interface
    ...
    function GetProvider: IProviderInterface;
```

```
  ...
  property Provider: IProviderInterface read GetProvider;

end;
```

2. In the ViewModel.Invoice unit, add the Model.ProSu.
Interfaces and Model.ProSu.Provider unit references,
declare a private variable in the TInvoiceViewModel class
to hold the provider class, and develop the method declared
in the interface of the class. In addition, add the code in the
constructor to initiate the provider class.

```
unit ViewModel.Invoice;

interface

...

implementation

uses
  ...
  Model.ProSu.Interfaces, Model.ProSu.Provider;

type
  TInvoiceViewModel = class(TInterfacedObject, IInvoiceViewModelInterface)
  private
    ...
    fProvider: IProSuProviderInterface;
    ...
    function GetProvider: IProviderInterface;
  public
    ...
  end;
...

constructor TInvoiceViewModel.Create;
begin
  ...
  fProvider:=CreateProSuProviderClass;
end;

function TInvoiceViewModel.GetProvider: IProviderInterface;
begin
  result:=fProvider;
end;
```

```
...
end.
```

   3.   In the View.InvoiceForm unit, add the following code.

```
unit View.InvoiceForm;

interface

...

type
  TSalesInvoiceForm = class(TForm)
    ...
  private
    ...
    fSubscriber: ISubscriberInterface;
    ...
  public
    ...
  end;

implementation

...

procedure TSalesInvoiceForm.SetViewModel(
  const newViewModel: IInvoiceViewModelInterface);
begin
  fViewModel:=newViewModel;
  if not Assigned(fViewModel) then
    raise Exception.Create('Sales Invoice View Model is required');
  fSubscriber:=CreateProSuSubscriberClass;
  fViewModel.Provider.Subscribe(fSubscriber);
  ...
end;
```

We have now a communication channel that starts from the ViewModel and ends to the View. Next, we need to retrieve the details of the customer who is selected in the customer popup box.

   4.   Go to Model.Declarations and create this record.

```
unit Model.Declarations

...
```

```
interface
...

type
  ...
  TCustomerDetailsText = record
    DiscountRate,
    OutstandingBalance: string;
  end;

implementation

end.
```

    5.   In `Model.Interfaces`, declare the `GetCustomer` procedure.

```
unit Model.Interfaces

...

interface

...
type
  ...
 IInvoiceModelInterface = interface
    ...
    procedure GetCustomer (const customerName: string; var customer:
TCustomer);
  end;

  IInvoiceViewModelInterface = interface
    ...
    procedure GetCustomerDetails (const customerName: string; var
customerDetails: TCustomerDetailsText);
  end;

implementation

end.
```

6. In Model.Invoice, develop the actual procedure.

```
unit Model.Invoice;

interface

...

implementation

uses
  ..., System.SysUtils;

type
  TInvoiceModel = class (TInterfacedObject, IInvoiceModelInterface)
  private
    ...
  public
    ...
   procedure GetCustomer (const customerName: string; var customer:
TCustomer);
  end;

...

procedure TInvoiceModel.GetCustomer(const customerName: string;
  var customer: TCustomer);
begin
  if trim(customerName)='' then
    customer:=nil
  else
  begin
    customer.ID:=fDatabase.GetCustomerFromName(trim(customerName)).ID;
    customer.Name:=fDatabase.GetCustomerFromName(trim(customerName)).Name;
customer.DiscountRate:=fDatabase.GetCustomerFromName(trim(customerName)).
DiscountRate;
customer.Balance:=fDatabase.GetCustomerFromName(trim(customerName)).Balance;

    fInvoice.CustomerID:=customer.ID;
  end;
end;

end.
```

109

7. In ViewModel.Invoice, retrieve the customer class and convert the data according to the View logic.

```
unit ViewModel.Invoice;

interface

...

implementation

...

type
  TInvoiceViewModel = class(TInterfacedObject, IInvoiceViewModelInterface)
  private
    ...
    procedure GetCustomerDetails (const customerName: string; var
customerDetails: TCustomerDetailsText);
  public
    ...
  end;

...
```

Here we implement the
View logic

```
procedure TInvoiceViewModel.GetCustomerDetails(const customerName: string;
  var customerDetails: TCustomerDetailsText);
var
  tmpCustomer: TCustomer;
begin
  if trim(customerName)='' then
  begin
    customerDetails.DiscountRate:='Please Choose a Customer';
    customerDetails.OutstandingBalance:='Please Choose a Customer';
  end
  else
  begin
    tmpCustomer:=TCustomer.Create;
    fModel.GetCustomer(trim(customerName), tmpCustomer);
    customerDetails.DiscountRate:=Format('%5.2f',
[tmpCustomer.DiscountRate])+'%';
    customerDetails.OutstandingBalance:=Format('%-n',[tmpCustomer.Balance]);
    tmpCustomer.Free;


    fInvoiceItemsEnabled:=true;
    fBalanceEnabled:=true;

  end;
end;

end.
```

8. Getting the labels for the components in the customer detail
    group box in View.InvoiceForm is very similar to initializing
    the text and captions of the InvoiceForm components. We
    write a new UpdateCustomerDetails procedure, which is
    initially called in SetupGUI to reset the fields. For this to
    work, I have declared a private fCustomerDetailsText field
    and move the uses declaration in the interface section.
    In addition, a method to reset the string grid is introduced
    (CleanInvoiceGrid).

```
unit View.InvoiceForm;

interface

uses
   ..., Model.Declarations;

type
  TSalesInvoiceForm = class(TForm)
    ...
  private
    ...
    fCustomerDetailsText: TCustomerDetailsText;
    ...
    procedure UpdateCustomerDetails;
  public
    ...
  end;

implementation

...

procedure TSalesInvoiceForm.SetupGUI;
...
begin
  ...
  fViewModel.GetCustomerDetails('', fCustomerDetailsText);
  UpdateCustomerDetails;
end;

procedure TSalesInvoiceForm.UpdateCustomerDetails;
begin
  LabelDiscountRateFigure.Text:=fCustomerDetailsText.DiscountRate;
  LabelTotalBalanceBig.Text:=fCustomerDetailsText.OutstandingBalance;

  CleanInvoiceGrid;
  UpdateGroups;
end;

end.
```

This initializes the
customer detail labels

The Model is the part of the design that accesses the persistent medium. Neither the ViewModel nor the View are aware how and from which sources datasets are retrieved. If you check the code of the GetCustomerDetails in the ViewModel, you can easily see that this is the part where we decide how information is going to be presented in the View. In other words, we have encapsulated the View logic of the information in the ViewModel. Similarly, the UpdateCustomerDetails method in the form is agnostic about the actual content of the fields to be presented and which group boxes should be activated, deactivated, or disabled; this is done at the ViewModel level.

Adding an Item to the Invoice

After a customer is selected, the user needs to add items in the invoice. We have a popup box menu with the items, a field for the quantity, and a button to add the item to the invoice. The added item appears in the string grid.

The Model

Managing the items of the invoice is part of the business logic and, thus, is the duty of the Model. Therefore, we need procedures to add an item to the invoice, to delete items, to retrieve the number of the items in an invoice, and to calculate the total amount of the invoice.

1. Add the following code in the IInvoiceModelInterface declaration in the Model.Interfaces unit.

```
IInvoiceModelInterface = interface
    ...
    procedure AddInvoiceItem(const itemDescription: string; const quantity:
integer);
    procedure GetInvoiceItems (var itemsList: TObjectList<TInvoiceItem>);
    procedure DeleteAllInvoiceItems;
    procedure CalculateInvoiceAmounts;
    function GetInvoiceRunningBalance:Currency;
    function GetNumberOfInvoiceItems: integer;
    property InvoiceRunningBalance: Currency read GetInvoiceRunningBalance;
    property NumberOfInvoiceItems: integer read GetNumberOfInvoiceItems;
  end;
```

2. Develop the code in the Model.Invoice unit.

```
type
  TInvoiceModel = class (TInterfacedObject, IInvoiceModelInterface)
  private
    ...
    fRunningBalance: Currency;
    function GetInvoiceRunningBalance:Currency;
    function GetNumberOfInvoiceItems: integer;
```

```
  public
    ...
    procedure AddInvoiceItem(const itemDescription: string; const quantity:
integer);
    procedure GetInvoiceItems (var itemsList: TObjectList<TInvoiceItem>);
    procedure GetInvoiceItemFromID (const itemID: Integer; var item: TItem);
    procedure DeleteAllInvoiceItems;
    procedure CalculateInvoiceAmounts;
 end;

...

procedure TInvoiceModel.AddInvoiceItem(const itemDescription: string; const
quantity: integer);
var
  tmpInvoiceItem: TInvoiceItem;
  tmpItem: TItem;
begin
  if trim(itemDescription)='' then
    Exit;

  tmpItem:=fDatabase.GetItemFromDescription(trim(itemDescription));
  if not Assigned(tmpItem) then
    Exit;

  tmpInvoiceItem:=TInvoiceItem.Create;
  tmpInvoiceItem.ID:=tmpItem.ID;
  tmpInvoiceItem.InvoiceID:=fInvoice.ID;
  tmpInvoiceItem.UnitPrice:=tmpItem.Price;
  tmpInvoiceItem.Quantity:=quantity;

  fCurrentInvoiceItems.Add(tmpInvoiceItem);

end;

procedure TInvoiceModel.GetInvoiceItems(
  var itemsList: TObjectList<TInvoiceItem>);
var
  tmpInvoiceItem: TInvoiceItem;
  i: integer;
begin
  if not Assigned(itemsList) then
    Exit;
  itemsList.Clear;
  for i:=0 to fCurrentInvoiceItems.Count-1 do
  begin
    tmpInvoiceItem:=TInvoiceItem.Create;
    tmpInvoiceItem.ID:=fCurrentInvoiceItems.Items[i].ID;
```

```
    tmpInvoiceItem.InvoiceID:=fCurrentInvoiceItems.Items[i].InvoiceID;
    tmpInvoiceItem.ItemID:=fCurrentInvoiceItems.Items[i].ItemID;
    tmpInvoiceItem.UnitPrice:=fCurrentInvoiceItems.Items[i].UnitPrice;
    tmpInvoiceItem.Quantity:=fCurrentInvoiceItems.Items[i].Quantity;

    itemsList.Add(tmpInvoiceItem);
  end;
end;

procedure TInvoiceModel.GetInvoiceItemFromID(const itemID: Integer;
  var item: TItem);
var
  tmpItem: TItem;
begin
  if not Assigned(item) then
    Exit;
  tmpItem:=fDatabase.GetItemFromID(itemID);
  if Assigned(tmpItem) then
  begin
    item.ID:=tmpItem.ID;
    item.Description:=tmpItem.Description;
    item.Price:=tmpItem.Price
  end;
end;

procedure TInvoiceModel.CalculateInvoiceAmounts;
var
  tmpItem: TInvoiceItem;
begin
  fRunningBalance:=0.00;
  for tmpItem in fCurrentInvoiceItems do
    fRunningBalance:=fRunningBalance+(tmpItem.Quantity*tmpItem.UnitPrice);
end;

function TInvoiceModel.GetInvoiceRunningBalance: Currency;
begin
  CalculateInvoiceAmounts;
  Result:=fRunningBalance;
end;

procedure TInvoiceModel.DeleteAllInvoiceItems;
begin
  fCurrentInvoiceItems.Clear;
end;

function TInvoiceModel.GetNumberOfInvoiceItems: integer;
begin
  result:=fCurrentInvoiceItems.Count;
end;
```

114

The ViewModel

1. Add and develop the following procedures in the Model.
    Interface and ViewModel.Invoice units.

```
unit Model.Interface;

implementation

...

type
  ...
  IInvoiceViewModelInterface = interface
    ...
    procedure AddInvoiceItem(const itemDescription: string; const quantity:
integer);
    procedure DeleteAllInvoiceItems;
  end;

implementation

end.

unit ViewModel.Invoice;

interface
...

implementation

...

type
  TInvoiceViewModel = class(TInterfacedObject, IInvoiceViewModelInterface)
  private
    ...
  public
    ...
    procedure AddInvoiceItem(const itemDescription: string; const quantity:
integer);
    procedure DeleteAllInvoiceItems;
  end;

procedure TInvoiceViewModel.AddInvoiceItem(const itemDescription: string;
  const quantity: integer);
begin
  fModel.AddInvoiceItem(itemDescription, quantity);
```

```
end;

procedure TInvoiceViewModel.DeleteAllInvoiceItems;
begin
  fModel.DeleteAllInvoiceItems;
end;
```

2. The ViewModel is doing all the required work to prepare the data into a form suitable for presentation. *Suitable* in this case means that the ViewModel should present the data to the View in such way that it could be shown in the string grid of the form. This illustrates the flexibility of the MVVM pattern; we use the ViewModel layer to adjust and manipulate the presentation state of the data according to the requirements of the View without the need to change the structural elements of the View (or the Model).

3. The string grid has five columns and receives strings. There are many ways to prepare data for this constellation. I will use a set of arrays that map to the columns of the string grid. Admittedly, this is not the best way to achieve this effect, but in this case, it is adequate as a demonstration of the functionality of the ViewModel.

4. Open Model.Declarations and add the following record.

```
unit Model.Declarations;

interface

...

type
  ...

  TInvoiceItemsText = record
    DescriptionText,
    QuantityText,
    UnitPriceText,
    PriceText,
    IDText: array of string;
    InvoiceRunningBalance,
    InvoiceTotalBalance: string;
  end;

implementation

end.
```

5. Declare a property and a getter function in the Model.
    Interfaces unit and write the code for the procedure in
    ViewModel.Invoice.

```
unit Model.Interfaces;

interface

...

type
  ...
  IInvoiceViewModelInterface = interface
    ...
    function GetInvoiceItemsText: TInvoiceItemsText;

    ...
    property InvoiceItemsText: TInvoiceItemsText read GetInvoiceItemsText;
  end;

implementation

end.

unit ViewModel.Invoice;

interface

...

implementation

uses
  ...

type
  TInvoiceViewModel = class(TInterfacedObject, IInvoiceViewModelInterface)
  private
    ...
    function GetInvoiceItemsText: TInvoiceItemsText;
  public
    ...
  end;

...

function TInvoiceViewModel.GetInvoiceItemsText: TInvoiceItemsText;
var
```

```
  tmpRunning: Currency;
  tmpInvoiceItems: TObjectList<TInvoiceItem>;
  i, tmpLen: integer;
  tmpItem: TItem;
begin
  tmpLen:=0;
  SetLength(fInvoiceItemsText.DescriptionText,tmpLen);
  SetLength(fInvoiceItemsText.QuantityText,tmpLen);
  SetLength(fInvoiceItemsText.UnitPriceText,tmpLen);
  SetLength(fInvoiceItemsText.PriceText,tmpLen);
  SetLength(fInvoiceItemsText.IDText, tmpLen);
  tmpRunning:=0.00;

    tmpInvoiceItems:=TObjectList<TInvoiceItem>.Create;
  fModel.GetInvoiceItems(tmpInvoiceItems);
  for i := 0 to tmpInvoiceItems.Count-1 do
  begin
    tmpLen:=Length(fInvoiceItemsText.DescriptionText)+1;
    SetLength(fInvoiceItemsText.DescriptionText,tmpLen);
    SetLength(fInvoiceItemsText.QuantityText,tmpLen);
    SetLength(fInvoiceItemsText.UnitPriceText,tmpLen);
    SetLength(fInvoiceItemsText.PriceText,tmpLen);
    SetLength(fInvoiceItemsText.IDText, tmpLen);

    tmpItem:=TItem.Create;
    fModel.GetInvoiceItemFromID(tmpInvoiceItems.Items[i].ID, tmpItem);
    fInvoiceItemsText.DescriptionText[tmpLen-1]:=tmpItem.Description;
    tmpItem.Free;

    fInvoiceItemsText.QuantityText[tmpLen-1]:=tmpInvoiceItems.Items[i].
    Quantity.ToString;
    fInvoiceItemsText.UnitPriceText[tmpLen-
    1]:=format('%10.2f',[tmpInvoiceItems.Items[i].UnitPrice]);
    fInvoiceItemsText.PriceText[tmpLen-1]:=
        format('%10.2f',[tmpInvoiceItems.Items[i].
        UnitPrice*tmpInvoiceItems.items[i].Quantity]);
    fInvoiceItemsText.IDText[tmpLen-1]:=tmpInvoiceItems.Items[i].ID.ToString;
  end;
  tmpInvoiceItems.Free;

  tmpRunning:=fModel.InvoiceRunningBalance;

  fInvoiceItemsText.InvoiceRunningBalance:=Format('%10.2f', [tmpRunning]);
  fInvoiceItemsText.InvoiceTotalBalance:=Format('%10.2f', [tmpRunning]);

  fPrintButtonEnabled:=fModel.NumberOfInvoiceItems > 0;

  Result:=fInvoiceItemsText;
end;
```

6.   The last procedure demonstrates the typical manipulation of data from the Model at the level of the ViewModel to represent the View logic. It also changes the status of the Print button to synchronize the View state with the state of the data.

The View

In the InvoiceForm, we need to retrieve the updated data from the ViewModel and present it in the form.

In View.InvoiceForm, declare a private variable called fInvoiceItemsText and add code to the click event of the Add button. We also need a procedure to update the items in the string grid (UpdateInvoiceGrid) and a procedure to update the total balances of the invoice (UpdateBalances). The following code (indicated in bold) also updates the SetViewModel procedure to call UpdateBalances in order to initialize the labels with the invoice's balances.

```
interface
...
type
  TSalesInvoiceForm = class(TForm)
    ...
    procedure ButtonAddItemClick(Sender: TObject);
  private
    ...
    procedure SetViewModel(
        const newViewModel: IInvoiceViewModelInterface);
    procedure UpdateBalances;
    procedure UpdateInvoiceGrid;
  public
    ...
  end;
...

implementation
...

procedure TSalesInvoiceForm.ButtonAddItemClick(Sender: TObject);
begin
  fViewModel.AddInvoiceItem(PopupBoxItems.Text,
EditQuantity.text.ToInteger);
end;

procedure TSalesInvoiceForm.UpdateInvoiceGrid;
var
  i: Integer;
begin
  StringGridItems.RowCount:=0;
  fInvoiceItemsText:=fViewModel.InvoiceItemsText;
  for i := 0 to Length(fInvoiceItemsText.DescriptionText)-1 do
```

```
begin
  StringGridItems.RowCount:=StringGridItems.RowCount+1;
    StringGridItems.Cells[0,StringGridItems.RowCount-
1]:=fInvoiceItemsText.DescriptionText[i];
    StringGridItems.Cells[1, StringGridItems.RowCount-
1]:=fInvoiceItemsText.QuantityText[i];
    StringGridItems.Cells[2, StringGridItems.RowCount-
1]:=fInvoiceItemsText.UnitPriceText[i];
    StringGridItems.Cells[3, StringGridItems.RowCount-
1]:=fInvoiceItemsText.PriceText[i];
    StringGridItems.Cells[4, StringGridItems.RowCount-
1]:=fInvoiceItemsText.IDText[i];
  end;
  UpdateBalances;
  UpdateGroups;
end;
```

We will update this later to include the discount

```
procedure TSalesInvoiceForm.UpdateBalances;
begin
  LabelRunningBalance.Text:=fInvoiceItemsText.InvoiceRunningBalance;
  LabelInvoiceBalance.Text:=fInvoiceItemsText.InvoiceTotalBalance;
  LabelTotalBalance.Text:=fInvoiceItemsText.InvoiceTotalBalance;
end;

procedure TSalesInvoiceForm.SetViewModel(
  const newViewModel: IInvoiceViewModelInterface);
begin
  fViewModel:=newViewModel;
  if not Assigned(fViewModel) then
    raise Exception.Create('Sales Invoice View Model is required');
  fSubscriber:=CreateProSuSubscriberClass;
  fViewModel.Provider.Subscribe(fSubscriber);
  UpdateLabels;
  SetupGUI;
  UpdateGroups;
  UpdatePrintingStatus;
  fInvoiceItemsText:=fViewModel.InvoiceItemsText;
  UpdateBalances;
end;
```

These two lines initialize the balance labels

The simplest way to update the grid with the invoice items is to call UpdateInvoiceGrid in the ButtonAddItemClick event. We are not going to follow this approach. Instead, we will ask the ViewModel to inform the View that there is a change to the invoice items and, therefore, it's time to refresh the string grid.

In order to achieve this effect, we will use the ProSu framework developed in Chapter 4.

1. Add an action (actInvoiceItemsChanged) in Model.ProSu. InterfaceActions to signify the need to update the grid with the invoice items.

```
unit Model.ProSu.InterfaceActions;

interface

type
  TInterfaceAction = (actUpdateTotalSalesFigure, actInvoiceItemsChanged);
  TInterfaceActions = set of TInterfaceAction;

implementation

end.
```

2. In View.InvoiceForm, declare a new procedure (NotificationFromProvider) that will be used to trigger actions from the message provider, register it with the provider, and write code to update the grid.

```
interface
...
type
  TSalesInvoiceForm = class(TForm)
    ...
    procedure ButtonAddItemClick(Sender: TObject);
  private
    ...
    procedure NotificationFromProvider (const notifyClass:
INotificationClass);
  public
    ...
  end;
...

implementation

uses
  ..., Model.ProSu.InterfaceActions;
...

procedure TSalesInvoiceForm.NotificationFromProvider(
  const notifyClass: INotificationClass);
var
  tmpNotifClass: TNotificationClass;
begin
  if notifyClass is TNotificationClass then
  begin
    tmpNotifClass:=notifyClass as TNotificationClass;
    if actInvoiceItemsChanged in tmpNotifClass.Actions then
      UpdateInvoiceGrid;
  end;
end;

procedure TSalesInvoiceForm.SetViewModel(
const newViewModel:IInvoiceViewModelInterface);       Add this line here
begin
  ...
  fSubscriber:=CreateProSuSubscriberClass;
  fSubscriber.SetUpdateSubscriberMethod(NotificationFromProvider);
  fViewModel.Provider.Subscribe(fSubscriber);
  ...
end;
```

3. In ViewModel.Invoice, create a new procedure to send out
   messages to subscribers (SendNotification). Call it from the
   AddInvoiceItem and DeleteAllInvoiceItems, as follows.

```
implementation

uses
  ..., Model.ProSu.InterfaceActions;

type
  TInvoiceViewModel = class(TInterfacedObject, IInvoiceViewModelInterface)
  private

    ...
    procedure SendNotification (const actions: TInterfaceActions);
  public

    ...
  end;

...

procedure TInvoiceViewModel.AddInvoiceItem(const itemDescription: string;
  const quantity: integer);
begin

  fModel.AddInvoiceItem(itemDescription, quantity);        Add this line here

  SendNotification([actInvoiceItemsChanged]);
end;

procedure TInvoiceViewModel.SendNotification(const actions:
TInterfaceActions);
var
  tmpNotificationClass: TNotificationClass;
begin
  tmpNotificationClass:=TNotificationClass.Create;
  try
    tmpNotificationClass.Actions:=actions;
    fProvider.NotifySubscribers(tmpNotificationClass);
  finally
    tmpNotificationClass.Free;
  end;
end;

procedure TInvoiceViewModel.DeleteAllInvoiceItems;
begin

  fModel.DeleteAllInvoiceItems;                             Add this line here
  endNotification([actInvoiceItemsChanged]);

end;
```

Compile POSApp and execute it. Choose a customer from the popup box. Select an item and try to add it to the invoice. You should be able to see that the grid updates the items and balances.

You may argue that there is no need to create the notification loop to get an update of the invoice items' grid in this View. We could very easily retrieve fViewModel. InvoiceItemsText in the View and publish the data. This is correct and it would work very well, too. The reason I chose to use ProSu here is because I wanted to show how the ViewModel (or the Model) could initiate communication.

For example, in a real application, we may have a situation in which item prices change in real-time due to availability and demand. Because of the way we constructed this application, we could easily implement this scenario. The ViewModel would send an actInvoiceItemsChanged to report on any updates even if the user was in the middle of issuing an invoice.

■ **Note**   There is a small glitch in the GUI at this stage. If you select a customer and add a few items to the invoice, you can see the balance. Selecting another customer from the popup box clears the grid, but doesn't initialize the balance. This is because we don't delete the invoice items from the Model. To fix this, add the following lines in the PopupBoxCustomerChange procedure in View.InvoiceForm.

```
procedure TSalesInvoiceForm.PopupBoxCustomerChange(Sender: TObject);
begin

   fViewModel.GetCustomerDetails(PopupBoxCustomer.Text,fCustomerDetailsText);
   fViewModel.DeleteAllInvoiceItems;
   PopupBoxItems.ItemIndex:=-1;
   UpdateCustomerDetails;
end;
```

Summary

We took some big steps in this chapter. We converted the most important parts of InvoiceForm in a way that builds boundaries between business logic, view state, and view logic. We also saw how the methodology we developed in the previous chapter, along with the tools and concepts we learned earlier in the book, all fit together to serve the purpose of MVVM design.

CHAPTER 7

Input Validation

The POSApp at this stage illustrates how we can use the MVVM pattern to capture user interaction. In this implementation, it doesn't perform any checks on data entered by the users. For example, users could enter a negative number or even a character in the quantity field. This will generate an error and will block the application. This chapter explains how we can deal with this situation.

Checking Inputs

This section shows how to check the user-entered data against three validation rules: users must select an item before they press the Add button, the quantity field must not be empty, and the quantity must be a non-zero positive number.

1. Use the project from the previous chapter (it's also found in the code files as POSAppMVVMUserInteraction) and add new types. They will identify errors in Model.ProSu. InterfaceActions and declare a new class to handle notifications for errors in Model.Declarations.

```
unit Model.ProSu.InterfaceActions;

interface

type
  ...
  TInterfaceError = (errInvoiceItemEmpty, errInvoiceItemQuantityEmpty,
                     errInvoiceItemQuantityNonPositive,
                     errInvoiceItemQuantityNotNumber, errNoError);
  TInterfaceErrors = set of TInterfaceError;

Implementation

end.

unit Model.Declarations;
```

```
interface

...

type
  ...
  TErrorNotificationClass = class (TInterfacedObject, INotificationClass)
  private
    fActions: TInterfaceErrors;
    fActionMessage: string;
  public
    property Actions: TInterfaceErrors read fActions write fActions;
    property ActionMessage: string read fActionMessage write fActionMessage;
  end;

implementation

end.
```

2. Add two procedures in the interface part of
IInvoiceViewModelInterface in Model.Interfaces. Both
procedures accept a string as an argument. We will pass
whatever the popup box and the edit field provide. Remember
that the View (InvoiceForm) is not (and should not be) aware
of the type of data users enter; in other words, the form does
not know that the quantity edit field must be a number.

```
IInvoiceViewModelInterface = interface
    ...
    procedure ValidateItem (const newItem: string);
    procedure ValidateQuantity (const newQuantityText: string);
end;
```

3. The ViewModel performs the checks on the strings. In bigger
and more complex applications, the Model can do validation
and perform checks as well.

4. Create a procedure in ViewModel.Invoice to send error
messages to subscribers.

```
type
  TInvoiceViewModel = class(TInterfacedObject, IInvoiceViewModelInterface)
  private
    ...
    procedure SendErrorNotification (const errorType: TInterfaceErrors;
                                     const errorMessage: string);
  public
    ...
  end;
...


procedure TInvoiceViewModel.SendErrorNotification (const errorType:
TInterfaceErrors;
                                                   const errorMessage: string);
var
  tmpErrorNotificationClass: TErrorNotificationClass;
begin
  tmpErrorNotificationClass:=TErrorNotificationClass.Create;
  try
    tmpErrorNotificationClass.Actions:=errorType;
    tmpErrorNotificationClass.ActionMessage:=errorMessage;
  fProvider.NotifySubscribers(tmpErrorNotificationClass);
  finally
    tmpErrorNotificationClass.Free;
  end;
end;
```

5.   Write the following code in the validation procedures.

```
procedure TInvoiceViewModel.ValidateItem(const newItem: string);
begin
  if trim(newItem)='' then
    SendErrorNotification([errInvoiceItemEmpty], 'Please choose an item')
  else
    SendErrorNotification([errNoError], '');
end;
```

```
procedure TInvoiceViewModel.ValidateQuantity(const newQuantityText: string);
var
  value,
  code: integer;
begin
  if trim(newQuantityText)='' then
  begin
    SendErrorNotification([errInvoiceItemQuantityEmpty], 'Please enter
quantity');
    Exit;
  end;

  Val(trim(newQuantityText), value, code);
  if code<>0 then
  begin
    SendErrorNotification([errInvoiceItemQuantityNotNumber], 'Quantity must
be a number');
    Exit;
  end;

  if trim(newQuantityText).ToInteger<=0 then
  begin
    SendErrorNotification([errInvoiceItemQuantityNonPositive],
                                      'The quantity must be positive
number');
    Exit;
  end;

  SendErrorNotification([errNoError], '');
end;
```

6. Now the only thing we need to do is process the error signals in View.InvoiceForm. We already have a procedure to manage signals from the provider (NotificationFromProvider); thus, we just update it accordingly.

```
procedure TSalesInvoiceForm.NotificationFromProvider(
  const notifyClass: INotificationClass);
var
  tmpNotifClass: TNotificationClass;
  tmpErrorNotifClass: TErrorNotificationClass;
begin
  if notifyClass is TNotificationClass then
  begin
    tmpNotifClass:=notifyClass as TNotificationClass;
    if actInvoiceItemsChanges in tmpNotifClass.Actions then      Add this code
      UpdateInvoiceGrid;
  end;
  if notifyClass is TErrorNotificationClass then
  begin
    tmpErrorNotifClass:=notifyClass as TErrorNotificationClass;
    if errInvoiceItemEmpty in tmpErrorNotifClass.Actions then
    begin
      ShowMessage(tmpErrorNotifClass.ActionMessage);
      PopupBoxItems.SetFocus;
      Exit;
    end
    else
    if errInvoiceItemQuantityEmpty in tmpErrorNotifClass.Actions then
    begin
      ShowMessage(tmpErrorNotifClass.ActionMessage);
      EditQuantity.SetFocus;
      Exit;
    end
    else
    if (errInvoiceItemQuantityNonPositive in tmpErrorNotifClass.Actions)
       or (errInvoiceItemQuantityNotNumber in tmpErrorNotifClass.Actions)
then
    begin
      ShowMessage(tmpErrorNotifClass.ActionMessage);
      EditQuantity.SelectAll;
      EditQuantity.SetFocus;
      Exit;
    end
    else
    begin

fViewModel.AddInvoiceItem(PopupBoxItems.Text,
EditQuantity.text.ToInteger);
    end;
  end;
end;
```

Add this code

This call will add the item to the invoice; see Step 7 for an explanation

7. In this design, the validation check reports on any errors by sending out an action that indicates an error (errInvoiceItemEmpty, errInvoiceItemQuantityEmpty, errInvoiceItemQuantityNonPositive, or errInvoiceItemQuantityNotNumber) or errNoError to show there is no error. The process takes place in the NotificationFromProvider procedure, so we must not add the item in the ButtonAddClick event. The process of adding the item is now handled by the NotificationFromProvider method.

```
procedure TSalesInvoiceForm.ButtonAddItemClick(Sender: TObject);
begin

  fViewModel.ValidateItem(PopupBoxItems.Text);
  fViewModel.ValidateQuantity(EditQuantity.Text);
end;
```

Add this code and remove the call to AddItem

Bits and Pieces

We have now completed the major tasks in the InvoiceForm. There are a few left before we have a fully rewritten version of the initial monolithic design of POSApp. These last tasks include a way to delete items from an invoice, apply discount to the total amount of the invoice, print the invoice and close the form.

Deleting an Item from the Invoice

When the user right-clicks on the invoice item list, a popup menu appears with an option to delete the selected item. In order to implement this functionality, follow the next steps:

1. Add DeleteInvoiceItem in IInvoiceModelInterface in Model.Interfaces.

```
IInvoiceModelInterface = interface
  ...
  procedure DeleteInvoiceItem (const delItemID: integer);
end;
```

2. Develop the procedure in Model.Invoice.

```
implementation

...

type
  TInvoiceModel = class (TInterfacedObject, IInvoiceModelInterface)
  private
    ...
```

```
  public
    ...
    procedure DeleteInvoiceItem (const delItemID: integer);
    ...
  end;

...

procedure TInvoiceModel.DeleteInvoiceItem(const delItemID: integer);
var
  i: integer;
begin
  if delItemID<=0 then
    Exit;
  for i := 0 to fCurrentInvoiceItems.Count-1 do
  begin
    if fCurrentInvoiceItems.Items[i].ID=delItemID then
    begin
      fCurrentInvoiceItems.Delete(i);
      break;
    end;
  end;
end;
```

3.   Back in Model.Interfaces, add a similar DeleteInvoiceItem
     for the ViewModel. Notice that this time, the procedure gets
     text as an argument because this is what the View can feed in
     to the ViewModel as it gets data from a string grid.

```
IInvoiceViewModelInterface = interface
    ...
    procedure DeleteInvoiceItem (const delItemIDAsText: string);
  end;
```

4.   In ViewModel.Invoice, add the code to DeleteInvoiceItem.

```
type
  TInvoiceViewModel = class(TInterfacedObject, IInvoiceViewModelInterface)
  private
    ...
  public
    ...
    procedure DeleteInvoiceItem (const delItemIDAsText: string);
  end;
...

procedure TInvoiceViewModel.DeleteInvoiceItem(const delItemIDAsText:
string);
```

131

```
begin
  if (trim(delItemIDAsText)='') then
    Exit;
  fModel.DeleteInvoiceItem(delItemIDAsText.ToInteger);
  SendNotification([actInvoiceItemsChanges]);
end;
```

5. In View.Invoice, we only need to call the DeleteInvoiceItem from the ViewModel. Then, the ViewModel will notify the View that there is a change to the invoice items and the balances.

6. Add an event handler to the MenuItemDeleteItem menu item of the PopupMenuItems popup menu component in View. InvoiceForm.

```
type
  TSalesInvoiceForm = class(TForm)
    ...
    procedure MenuItemDeleteItemClick(Sender: TObject);
  private
    ...
  public
    ...
  end;

...

procedure TSalesInvoiceForm.MenuItemDeleteItemClick(Sender: TObject);
begin

  if (StringGridItems.Selected>=0) and
      (StringGridItems.Selected<=StringGridItems.RowCount-1) then
    fViewModel.DeleteInvoiceItem(StringGridItems.Cells[4, StringGridItems.
Selected]);
end;
```

Applying Discounts to the Invoices

The discount check box signals POSApp to apply the customer discount, which then appears in the top part of the form. We will implement this functionality by declaring a property in the ViewModel and the Model and changing the ViewModel's property from the View.

1. Declare a property in Model.Interfaces for the IInvoiceModelInterface and IInvoiceViewModelInterface.

```
IInvoiceModelInterface = interface
    ...
```

```
    function GetInvoiceDiscount: Currency;
    ...
    property InvoiceDiscount: Currency read GetInvoiceDiscount;
  end;

IInvoiceViewModelInterface = interface
    ...
    procedure SetDiscountApplied (const discount: boolean);
    function GetDiscountApplied: boolean;
    ...
    property DiscountApplied: boolean read GetDiscountApplied write
SetDiscountApplied;
end;
```

> 2. Add the code for the procedure and the function in the
>   ViewModel.Invoice unit.

```
type
  TInvoiceViewModel = class(TInterfacedObject, IInvoiceViewModelInterface)
  private
    ...
    fDiscountChecked: boolean;
    ...
    procedure SetDiscountApplied (const discount: boolean);
    function GetDiscountApplied: boolean;
  public
    ...
  end;
...

function TInvoiceViewModel.GetDiscountApplied: boolean;
begin
  result:=fDiscountChecked;
end;

procedure TInvoiceViewModel.SetDiscountApplied(const discount: boolean);
begin
  fDiscountChecked:=discount;
end;
```

> 3. In Model.Declarations, add a field to TInvoiceItemsText.

```
TInvoiceItemsText = record
    ...
    InvoiceDiscountFigure,
    InvoiceTotalBalance: string;
  end;
```

4. Develop the procedures declared in the Model.Invoice unit. Notice the auxiliary procedure, which provides the customer record based on customerID (GetCustomerFromID).

```
type
  TInvoiceModel = class (TInterfacedObject, IInvoiceModelInterface)
  private
    ...
    fDiscount: Currency;
    procedure GetCustomerFromID (const customerID: integer; var customer:
TCustomer);
    function GetInvoiceDiscount: Currency;
  public
    ...
  end;

...

procedure TInvoiceModel.GetCustomerFromID(const customerID: integer;
  var customer: TCustomer);
var
  tmpCustomerList: TObjectList<TCustomer>;
  tmpCustomer: TCustomer;
begin
  if not Assigned(customer) then
    Exit;
  GetCustomerList(tmpCustomerList);
  for tmpCustomer in tmpCustomerList do
    if tmpCustomer.ID=customerID then
    begin
      customer.ID:=tmpCustomer.ID;
      customer.Name:=tmpCustomer.Name;
      customer.DiscountRate:=tmpCustomer.DiscountRate;
      customer.Balance:=tmpCustomer.Balance;
      break;
    end;
end;
...
```

tmpCustomerList is directly managed by GetCustomerList

5. In ViewModel.Invoice, we need to develop the getter and setter of the DiscountApplied property. We also need to update the GetInvoiceItemsText function to include the discount in the calculations.

```
type
  TInvoiceViewModel = class(TInterfacedObject, IInvoiceViewModelInterface)
  private
    ...
    procedure SetDiscountApplied (const discount: boolean);
    function GetDiscountApplied: boolean;
```

```
  public
    ...
  end;

  ...

function TInvoiceViewModel.GetDiscountApplied: boolean;
begin
  result:=fDiscountChecked;
end;

procedure TInvoiceViewModel.SetDiscountApplied(const discount: boolean);
begin
  fDiscountChecked:=discount;
end;

function TInvoiceViewModel.GetInvoiceItemsText: TInvoiceItemsText;
var
  ...
  tmpDiscount: Currency;
begin
  ...
  tmpRunning:=0.00;
  tmpDiscount:=0.00;

  tmpInvoiceItems:=TObjectList<TInvoiceItem>.Create;
  fModel.GetInvoiceItems(tmpInvoiceItems);
  for i := 0 to tmpInvoiceItems.Count-1 do
  begin
    tmpLen:=Length(fInvoiceItemsText.DescriptionText)+1;
    SetLength(fInvoiceItemsText.DescriptionText,tmpLen);
    SetLength(fInvoiceItemsText.QuantityText,tmpLen);
    SetLength(fInvoiceItemsText.UnitPriceText,tmpLen);
    SetLength(fInvoiceItemsText.
PriceText,tmpLen);    SetLength(fInvoiceItemsText.IDText, tmpLen);

    tmpItem:=TItem.Create;
    fModel.GetInvoiceItemFromID(tmpInvoiceItems.Items[i].ID, tmpItem);
    fInvoiceItemsText.DescriptionText[tmpLen-1]:=tmpItem.Description;
    tmpItem.Free;

    fInvoiceItemsText.QuantityText[tmpLen-1]:=tmpInvoiceItems.Items[i].
    Quantity.ToString;
    fInvoiceItemsText.UnitPriceText[tmpLen-
1]:=format('%10.2f',[tmpInvoiceItems.Items[i].UnitPrice]);
    fInvoiceItemsText.PriceText[tmpLen-1]:=
        format('%10.2f',[tmpInvoiceItems.Items[i].UnitPrice*tmpInvoiceItems.
        items[i].Quantity]);
```

```
    fInvoiceItemsText.IDText[tmpLen-1]:=tmpInvoiceItems.Items[i].ID.ToString;
  end;
  tmpInvoiceItems.Free;

  tmpRunning:=fModel.InvoiceRunningBalance;

  if fDiscountChecked then
    tmpDiscount:=fModel.InvoiceDiscount;

  fInvoiceItemsText.InvoiceRunningBalance:=Format('%10.2f', [tmpRunning]);
  fInvoiceItemsText.InvoiceDiscountFigure:=Format('%10.2f', [tmpDiscount]);
  fInvoiceItemsText.InvoiceTotalBalance:=Format('%10.2f', [tmpRunning-
  tmpDiscount]);

  fPrintButtonEnabled:=fModel.NumberOfInvoiceItems > 0;

  Result:=fInvoiceItemsText;
end;
```

> 6. Move to View.InvoiceForm and write the change event of
>   the CheckBoxDiscount. Then update the UpdateBalances to
>   include the discount figure and the status of the check box.

```
type
  TSalesInvoiceForm = class(TForm)
    ...
    procedure CheckBoxDiscountChange(Sender: TObject);
  private
    ...
  public
    ...
  end;
...

procedure TSalesInvoiceForm.CheckBoxDiscountChange(Sender: TObject);
begin
  fViewModel.DiscountApplied:=CheckBoxDiscount.IsChecked;
  fInvoiceItemsText:=fViewModel.InvoiceItemsText;
  UpdateBalances;
end;

procedure TSalesInvoiceForm.UpdateBalances;
begin
  ...
  LabelDiscount.Text:=fInvoiceItemsText.InvoiceDiscountFigure;
  CheckBoxDiscount.IsChecked:=fViewModel.DiscountApplied;
end;
```

Compile the project and execute it. Add a customer who has a discount, add a few items, and check and uncheck the discount check box. You should be able to see that the amount is updated.

Printing the Invoice and Closing the Form

When the user attempts to print an invoice, the ViewModel changes the visibility of the animated indicator and the printing label and pushes the request to the Model. Then, the ViewModel informs the View that the process is complete. A confirmation message appears and the invoice form sends a message to the main form to update the sales figure. Eventually, the form closes. Once again, the starting point is the interface declarations.

1. In Model.Interfaces, declare two identical procedures (PrintInvoice), one for the Model and one for the ViewModel.

```
IInvoiceModelInterface = interface
   ...
   procedure PrintInvoice;
 end;

IInvoiceViewModelInterface = interface
   ...
   procedure PrintInvoice;
end;
```

2. Implement PrintInvoice in the Model.Invoice unit.

```
type
  TInvoiceModel = class (TInterfacedObject, IInvoiceModelInterface)
  private
    ...
    procedure PrintInvoice;
  public
    ...
  end;
...
procedure TInvoiceModel.PrintInvoice;
begin
  fDatabase.SaveCurrentSales(fRunningBalance-fDiscount);
end;
```

3. Based on the original POSApp developed in Chapter 2, we want the animated indicator and printing label to appear when the user prints an invoice. In the MVVM design, this means that the View needs to know when to update the status of the controls, which is received from the ViewModel. Once again, the ProSu framework developed earlier is handy here. The ViewModel will notify the View to update the status of the components.

4. A similar behavior is expected after the invoice has been printed. We need to declare a new interface action in Model. ProSu.InterfaceActions, as follows.

```
type
  TInterfaceAction = (actUpdateTotalSalesFigure, actInvoiceItemsChanges,
                      actPrintingStart, actPrintingFinish);
```

Add these

5. The ViewModel.Invoice unit manipulates the state of the View, accesses the Model, and implements the View logic.

```
type
  TInvoiceViewModel = class(TInterfacedObject, IInvoiceViewModelInterface)
  public
    ...
    procedure PrintInvoice;
  end;
...

procedure TInvoiceViewModel.PrintInvoice;
var
  tmpNotifClass: TNotificationClass;
begin
  fAniIndicatorVisible:=true;
  fPrintingLabelVisible:=true;

  SendNotification([actPrintingStart]);

  fModel.PrintInvoice;

  fAniIndicatorVisible:=false;
  fPrintingLabelVisible:=false;

  SendNotification([actPrintingFinish]);
end;
```

Change of view state before the printing

Inform the View

Access to the Model

Change of View state after printing

Notify the View about the change of View state

6. In View.Invoice, we process the notifications in the NotificationFromProvider procedure and write the PrintInvoice click event.

```
type
  TSalesInvoiceForm = class(TForm)
    ...
    procedure ButtonPrintInvoiceClick(Sender: TObject);
  private
    ...
  end;
...

procedure TSalesInvoiceForm.ButtonPrintInvoiceClick(Sender: TObject);
begin
  fViewModel.PrintInvoice;
end;
...

procedure TSalesInvoiceForm.NotificationFromProvider(
  const notifyClass: INotificationClass);
...
begin
  if notifyClass is TNotificationClass then
  begin
    tmpNotifClass:=notifyClass as TNotificationClass;
    if actInvoiceItemsChanges in tmpNotifClass.Actions then
      UpdateInvoiceGrid;

    if actPrintingStart in tmpNotifClass.Actions then
    begin
      AniIndicatorProgress.Visible:=fViewModel.AniIndicatorProgressVisible;
      LabelPrinting.Visible:=fViewModel.LabelPrintingVisible;
    end;

    if actPrintingFinish in tmpNotifClass.Actions then
    begin
      ShowMessage('Invoice Printed');
      AniIndicatorProgress.Visible:=fViewModel.AniIndicatorProgressVisible;
      LabelPrinting.Visible:=fViewModel.LabelPrintingVisible;
      self.Close;
    end;
  end;
...
end;
```

7. The last thing we need to do is update the total sales figure in the MainForm. This time, the InvoiceForm sends a message to the MainForm to perform the update. In the ProSu design, the InvoiceForm is the provider and the MainForm plays the role of the subscriber.

8. In View.InvoiceForm, add the following code. We also need to declare Model.ProSu.Provider in the uses clause.

```
type
  TSalesInvoiceForm = class(TForm)
    ...
  private
    ...
    fProvider: IProviderInterface
    ...
    procedure UpdateMainBalance;
  public
    property Provider: IProviderInterface read fProvider;
  end;
...
implementation

uses
    ..., Model.ProSu.Provider;
...

procedure TSalesInvoiceForm.NotificationFromProvider(
  const notifyClass: INotificationClass);
...
begin
  if notifyClass is TNotificationClass then
  begin
    tmpNotifClass:=notifyClass as TNotificationClass;
    if actInvoiceItemsChanges in tmpNotifClass.Actions then
      UpdateInvoiceGrid;

    if actPrintingStart in tmpNotifClass.Actions then
    begin
      AniIndicatorProgress.Visible:=fViewModel.AniIndicatorProgressVisible;
      LabelPrinting.Visible:=fViewModel.LabelPrintingVisible;
    end;

    if actPrintingFinish in tmpNotifClass.Actions then
    begin
      ShowMessage('Invoice Printed');
      AniIndicatorProgress.Visible:=fViewModel.AniIndicatorProgressVisible;
```

```
    LabelPrinting.Visible:=fViewModel.LabelPrintingVisible;
    UpdateMainBalance;
    self.Close;
  end;
end;
...
end;
...

procedure TSalesInvoiceForm.SetViewModel(
  const newViewModel: IInvoiceViewModelInterface);
begin
  ...
  fProvider:=CreateProSuProviderClass;
end;
procedure TSalesInvoiceForm.UpdateMainBalance;
var
  tmpNotificationClass: TNotificationClass;
begin
  tmpNotificationClass:=TNotificationClass.Create;
  tmpNotificationClass.Actions:=[actUpdateTotalSalesFigure];
  if Assigned(fProvider) then
   fProvider.NotifySubscribers(tmpNotificationClass);
  tmpNotificationClass.Free;
end;
```

9. Finally, in View.MainForm, subscribe the form to the InvoiceForm's provider and retrieve the total sales figure directly from the ViewModel.

```
procedure TMainForm.ButtonInvoiceClick(Sender: TObject);
...
begin
  invoiceModel:=CreateInvoiceModelClass;
  invoiceViewModel:=CreateInvoiceViewModelClass;
  invoiceViewModel.Model:=invoiceModel;

  tmpInvoiceForm:=TSalesInvoiceForm.Create(self);
  tmpInvoiceForm.ViewModel:=invoiceViewModel;
  tmpInvoiceForm.Provider.Subscribe(fSubscriber);
  try
    tmpInvoiceForm.ShowModal;
  finally
    tmpInvoiceForm.Free;
  end;
end;
...
```

141

```
procedure TMainForm.NotificationFromProvider(
   const notifyClass: INotificationClass);
 var
   tmpNotifClass: TNotificationClass;
 begin
   if notifyClass is TNotificationClass then
   begin
     tmpNotifClass:=notifyClass as TNotificationClass;
     if actUpdateTotalSalesFigure in tmpNotifClass.Actions then

     LabelTotalSalesFigure.Text:=fViewModel.GetTotalSalesValue;
   end;
 end;
```

Replace
LabelTotalSalesFigure. Text:=format('%10.2f',[tmpNotifClass
.ActionValue]);
with this

The final touch is to create the event for the Cancel button. This is a straightforward call to close the View.InvoiceForm.

```
type
  TSalesInvoiceForm = class(TForm)
    ...
    procedure ButtonCancelClick(Sender: TObject);
  private
    ...
  end;
...

procedure TSalesInvoiceForm.ButtonCancelClick(Sender: TObject);
begin
  self.Close;
end;
```

Summary

We have now completed the development of POSApp under the MVVM approach. In this chapter, we moved one step ahead from user interaction and saw how the MVVM paradigm, the ProSu pattern, and the bi-directional exchange of messages among the components of MVVM can help validate user input. We implemented different types of validations and evaluated how the View and ViewModel can sync when we need to complete processes involving different steps, such as when printing an invoice.

Index

A, B, C, D, E, F, G, H

Concept2 performance monitor, 9–10

I, J, K

Invoice form
deleting an item
model, 112–114
view, 119–124
viewmodel, 115–119
dummy variables, 79–81
model, 82–84, 91
setting up, 90–97
view, 79–81, 89
viewmodel, 85–86, 89, 96

L

Legacy code, 13

M, N

Main form
dummy variables, 44, 51, 53
model, 45–48, 53–55
view, 43–45, 65
viewmodel, 48–51, 53–56
Model-View-ViewModel (MVVM)
disabling and hiding
elements, 98–101
input validation, 125–142
two-way communication, 59–77
user interaction, 8, 103, 105–125, 142
Monolithic design, 13, 22

O

Observer pattern, 60, 65, 77

P, Q, R

Presentation patterns
MVC, 3–5
MVP, 6–7
MVVM, 7–11, 22
Provider-Subscriber (ProSu) Framework,
60–65, 68, 71, 77, 105, 121, 138

S

Separation of concerns (SoC), 1, 2, 5

T, U

3-tier application architecture
business layer, 2, 7, 10
data access layer, 2
presentation layer, 2, 10
3-tier application architecture
and MVC, 3–7
3-tier application architecture and MVP, 6–8
3-tier application architecture and
MVVM, 7–11

V, W, X, Y, Z

View-logic, 8, 43, 48, 56–57, 110, 112, 119,
124, 138
View state, 8, 42–43, 48, 56–57, 93,
98, 119, 124

© John Kouraklis 2016
J. Kouraklis, *MVVM in Delphi*, DOI 10.1007/978-1-4842-2214-0

Get the eBook for only $5!

Why limit yourself?

Now you can take the weightless companion with you wherever you go and access your content on your PC, phone, tablet, or reader.

Since you've purchased this print book, we're happy to offer you the eBook in all 3 formats for just $5.

Convenient and fully searchable, the PDF version enables you to easily find and copy code—or perform examples by quickly toggling between instructions and applications. The MOBI format is ideal for your Kindle, while the ePUB can be utilized on a variety of mobile devices.

To learn more, go to www.apress.com/companion or contact support@apress.com.